Joachim Klang • Uwe Kurth

BRICKS & TRICKS

THE NEW BIG UNOFFICIAL LEGO® BUILDERS BOOK

HEEL

I'm a big fan of the movies and they often inspire my constructions, so I'm dedicating this book to the *cinema* magazine.

■ ACKNOWLEDGMENTS

Thanks to the many pioneers and revolutionaries, some of whom we know personally and admire:

2LegoOrNot2Lego	Gambort	Misterzumbi
Aaaron Newman	gearcs	Nannan Z
Arvo Brothers	Grantmasters	NENN
ArzLan	Henrik Hoexbroe	Norton74
Bart Willen	Homa	Obedient Machine
Ben®	Joe Meno	Ochre Jelly
Brian Corredor	Jojo	„Orion Pax"
Bricksonwheels	Jonathan Elliott	Paul Vermeesch
Brickthing	Karwik	Pepa Quin
Bricktrix	Kevin Hall	_pixeljunkie_
Bruceywan	Lazer Blade	RoccoB
Cale Leiphart	lego_nabii	Sir Nadroj
captainsmog	Legohaulic	Sirens-Of-Titan
Colognebrick	LEGOLAS	Spencer_R
Cole Blaq	Legonardo Davidy	T.Oechsner
Cuahchic	Legopard	Taz-Maniac
DecoJim	Legotrucks	ted @ndes
- Derfel Cadarn -	_lichtblau_	TheBrickAvenger
Digger1221	‚LL'	Théolego
Drivebrick	Maciej Drwiega	tnickolaus
Eastpole77	Mark of Falworth	Toltomeja
Fianat	markus19840420	x_Speed
Fraslund	marshal banana	Xenomurphy
Fredoichi	McBricker	
Gabe Umland	Mijasper	

As always, thanks are due to coauthor Lutz Uhlmann for digitizing the constructions. Thanks are of course also due to the LDraw.org-Community for the programs that help us create the assembly instructions.

HEEL Verlag GmbH
Gut Pottscheidt
53639 Königswinter
Germany
Tel.: +49 (0) 2223 9230-0
Fax: +49 (0) 2223 9230-13
E-Mail: info@heel-verlag.de
www.heel-verlag.de

© 2018 HEEL Verlag GmbH

Authors Joachim Klang and Uwe Kurth
Layout and Illustration: Odenthal Illustration, www.odenthal-illustration.de
Photography: Thomas Schultze, www.thomas-schultze.de
Translated from German by: Laila Friese in association with First Edition Translations Ltd, Cambridge, UK
Edited by: Robert Anderson in association with First Edition Translations Ltd, Cambridge, UK
Project management: Ulrike Reihn-Hamburger

Printed in Slovenia

ISBN 978-3-95843-762-3

▮CONTENT

▮FOREWORD

It can sometimes feel like there's an endless variety of LEGO® bricks available. Almost every month there are new shapes and colors, producing a wealth of choice you can't fail to notice. In among the new pieces are also parts that fans like me have waited for patiently for years. That's why I think it's important to show you all the different ways you can use these new bricks. Naturally, we also want to focus on some of the well-established but little-noticed building blocks that may have been forgotten, but also have tremendous potential, and which we hadn't introduced in our *"Tips, Tricks and Building Techniques for LEGO® Bricks"* book.

The different ways you can use some LEGO® parts is not always obvious. When I was rooting around my collection, for example, I suddenly had an old boat weight in my hand. The shape immediately reminded me of spaceship models from the 1950s, and lo and behold a new use for it as well as a first idea for this book were born.

If you have lots of ideas for your own projects, but no way to implement them, newly released bricks or parts can really help. And as a rule—the smaller the better. Some really useful elements have been produced recently. New elements offering yet more possibilities have even been released since I started writing these lines. After all, the world of LEGO® isn't just made up of 2x4 bricks.

In the past, I have often heard of or read the description "special bricks"—mostly as a criticism. But if you take a closer look, every brick is special. It's always a question of what you use it for. Of course, some bricks are a bit rarer than others as they can't be found in all sets, and it is often these bricks that make models come alive. Of course, I know what people mean by "special bricks." At some of our exhibitions, to our general amazement, visitors have said some quite extraordinary things in conversation. One visitor, for example, exclaimed: "But these bricks have been manufactured specially for you." This couldn't be further from the truth! For me, it's a particular thrill to build my own models using only officially available elements.

Since I always try to construct my models as realistically and in as much detail as possible, I often have to buy new sets myself or look for particular bricks online. While my collection is relatively large, it can never be complete. So, if I want to use a certain brick in a particular color, I have to look hard to find it. Sometimes these are quite common bricks that you probably have in your box, but it may be that I've already used them in a different model.

So I hope you're looking forward to browsing the next few pages: perhaps you'll discover some new ideas that you can use for your own models.

INTRODUCTION

One of our earlier titles in our Tricks for Bricks series was well received by you. We have had so many positive responses that we thought it was time for the next one.

This time we are focusing entirely on the elements themselves. We look at some of the bricks that we find particularly useful and try to develop our ideas based on these bricks in order to showcase their versatility. But of course we also have some concrete instructions for new models.

To help you allocate or find the pieces we mention we always give you the LEGO® part number and the BrickLink (BL) number. Since LEGO® often assigns new numbers when items have not been available

in sets for a long time, these numbers may vary or be missing.

Our first update, which you can already see on this double page, is some alternative construction proposals for our Plymouth Belvedere. You've already seen the original instructions in Tips, Tricks and Building Techniques. We are constantly changing, expanding, and improving our models—or "mocs" (my own creation). But sometimes we also develop a model together, and we call these "occs" (our collective creation).

You can also find our models on Instagram (#_derjoe_ or # der_beueler) or Flickr (-derjoe or Der Beueler).

NICE PART USAGE

You can see how versatile some LEGO® elements can be in the example of this spaceship. Its design is inspired by classic science fiction. I think the boat weights work really well as engines on the elevator and on the wings.

■ SPACESHIP

It's an emergency landing by a spaceship on an alien planet; the hapless crew is trying to sort out the problem. Perhaps there's a helping hand around the next corner …

Beyond the instructions, you can decorate the model with stickers from old LEGO® sets. Or you can make the model using different colors; the weights are also available in black. It's also the weights that make the model heavy: at 7oz or more, it weighs much more than usual LEGO® models.

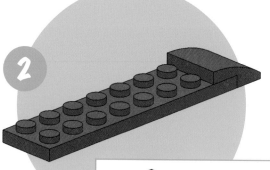

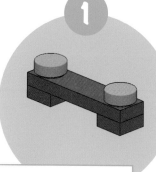

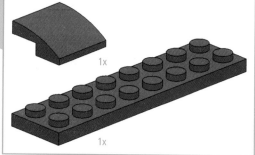

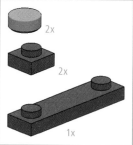

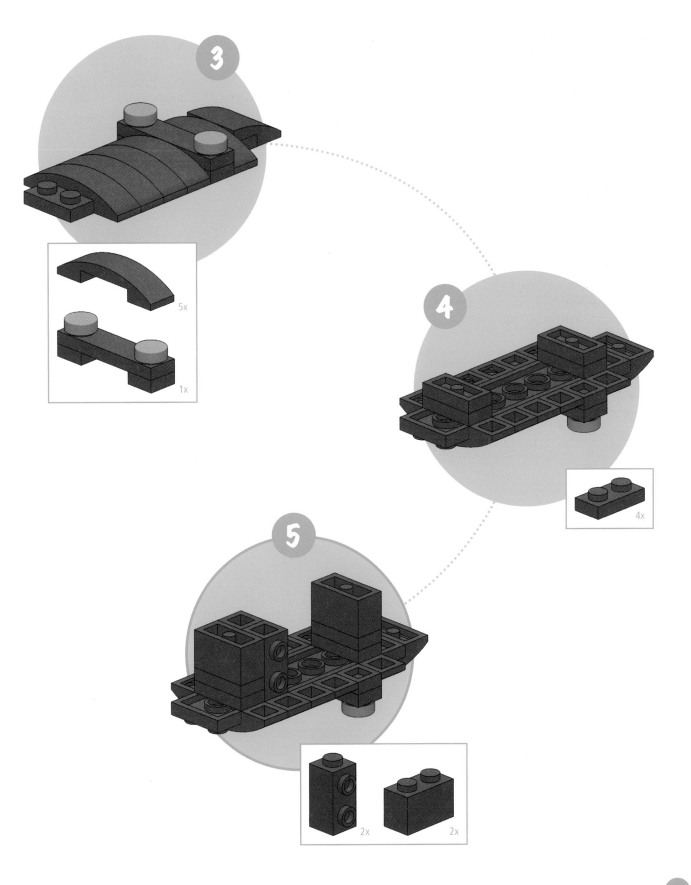

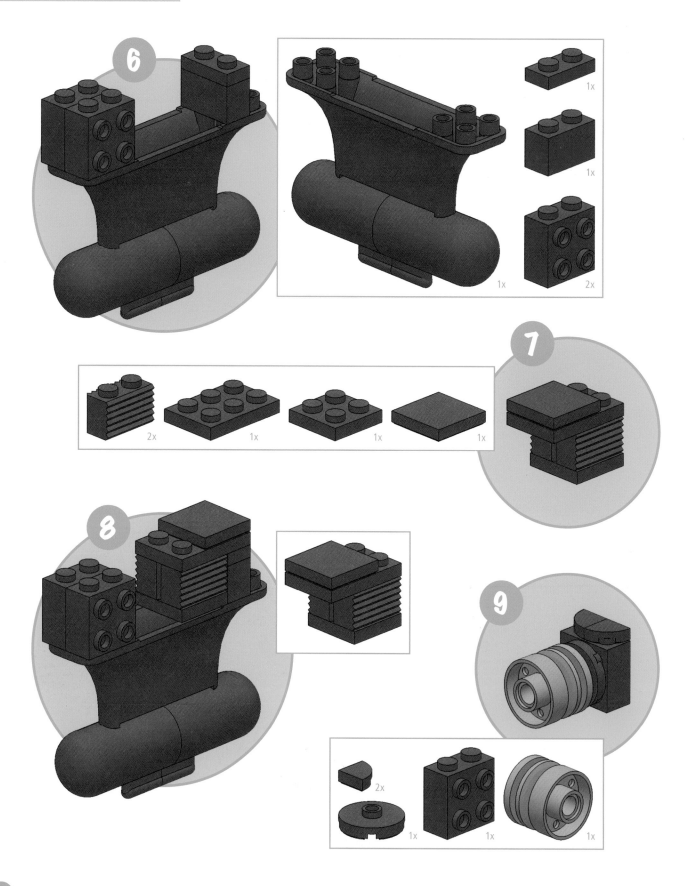

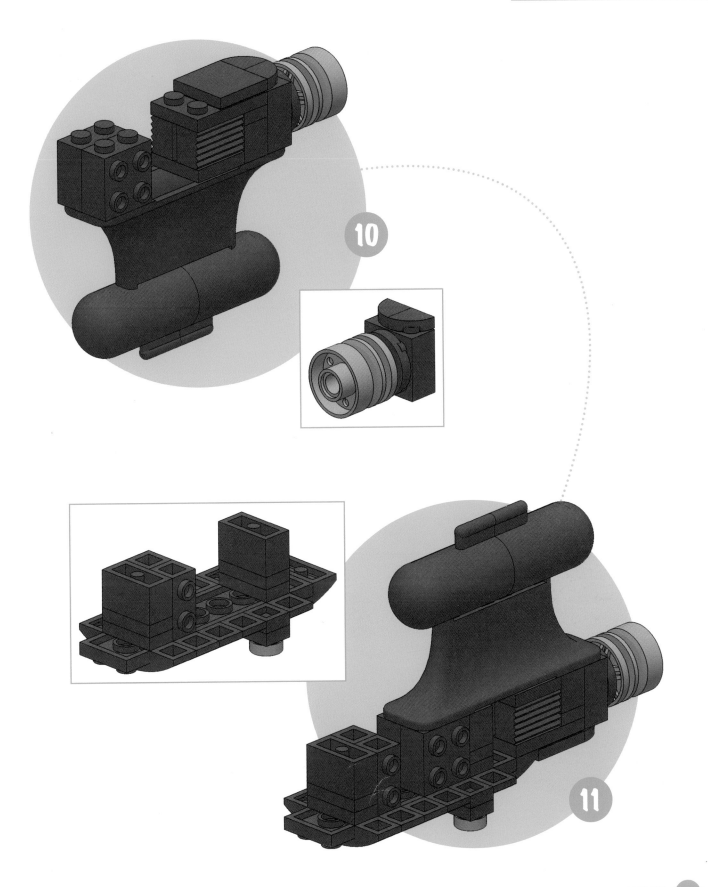

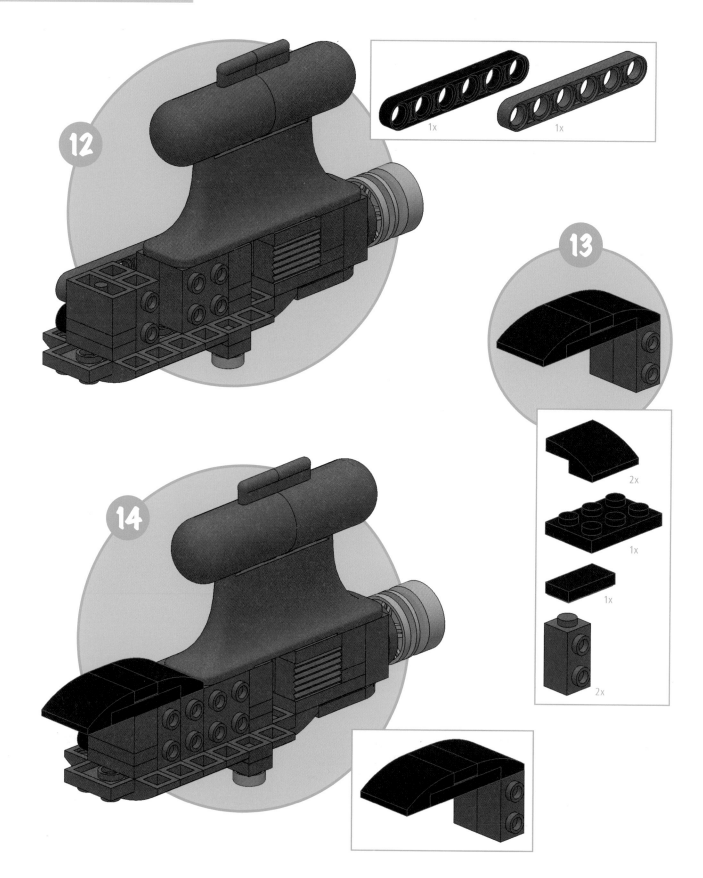

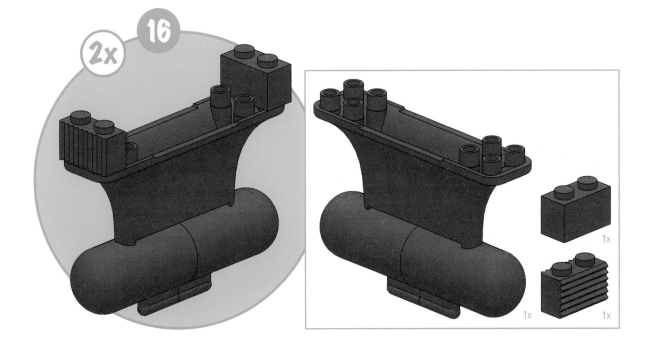

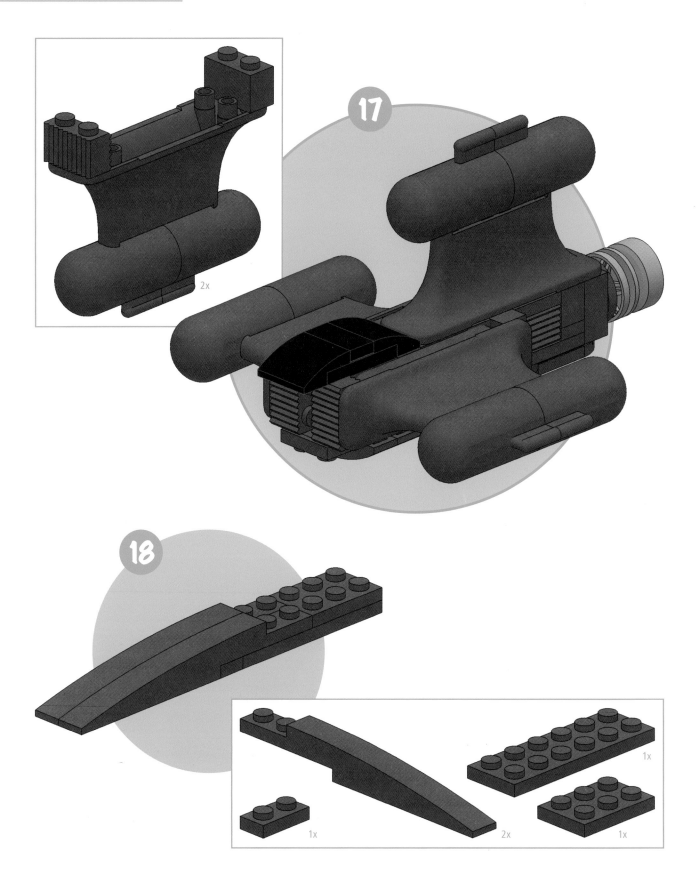

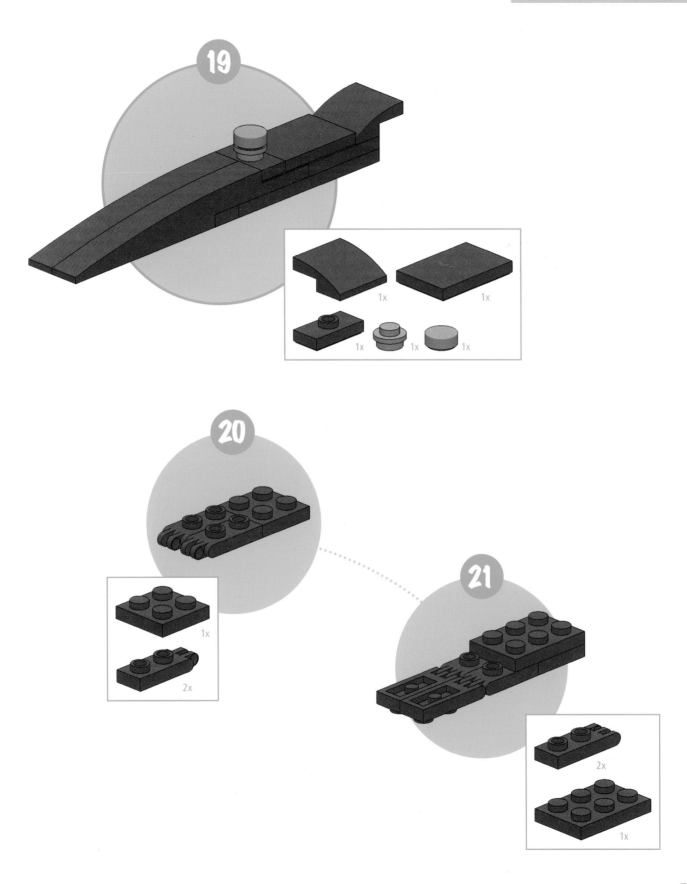

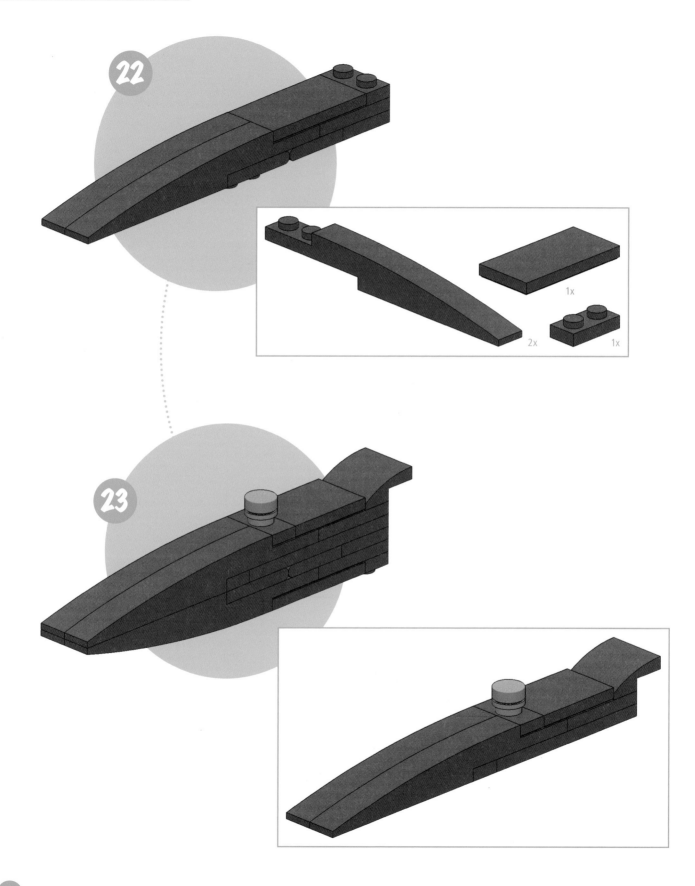

22

2x   1x   1x

23

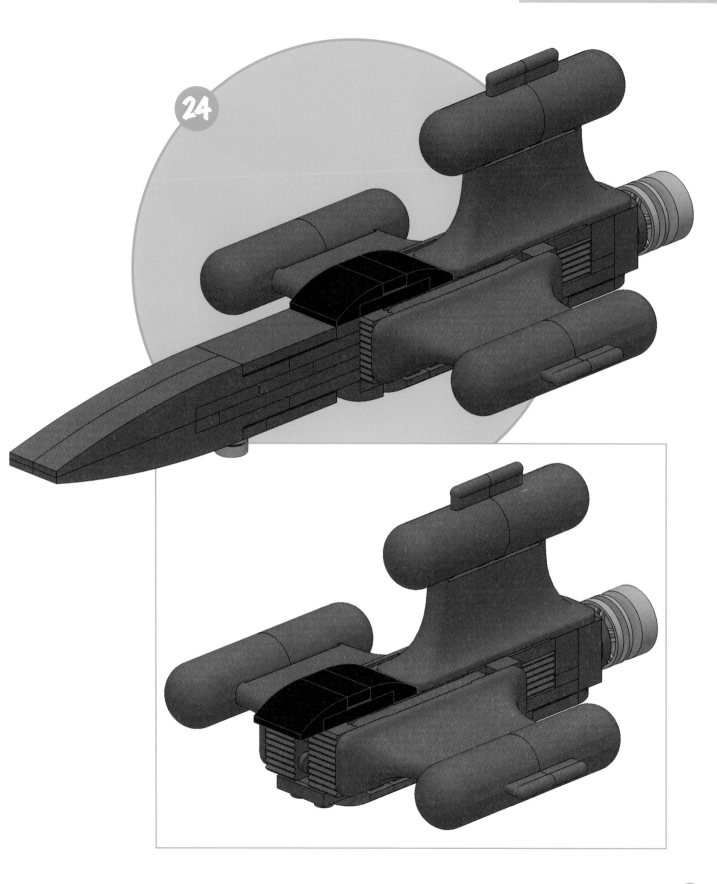

■PARTS LIST

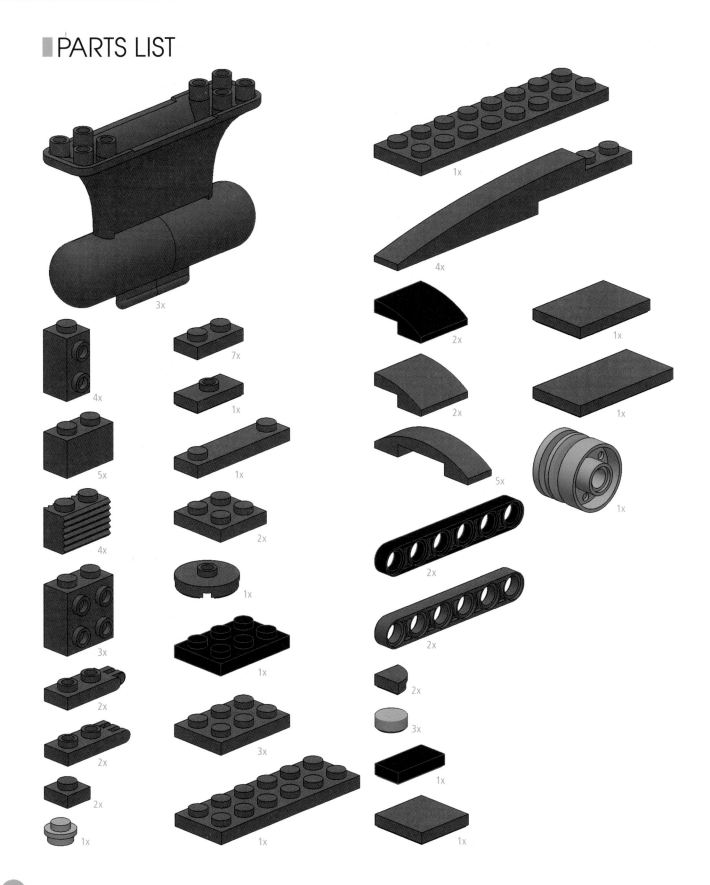

3x

1x

4x

4x

7x

2x

1x

5x

1x

2x

1x

5x

1x

4x

1x

2x

5x

1x

3x

1x

2x

2x

1x

2x

3x

2x

1x

3x

2x

1x

1x

1x

1x

Amount	Color	Part number	Name	LEGO® Part number
3	Red	u9308	Boat Keel Weighted 2 x 8 x 4 with Bottom Tab	
4	Red	32952	Brick 1 x 1 x 1.667 with Studs on 1 Side	6187620
5	Red	3004	Brick 1 x 2	300421, 4613961
4	Red	2877	Brick 1 x 2 with Grille	287721
3	Red	22885	Brick 1 x 2 x 1.667 with Studs on 1 Side	6135130
2	Red	4276	Hinge Plate 1 x 2 with 2 Fingers and Hollow Studs	
2	Red	4275	Hinge Plate 1 x 2 with 3 Fingers and Hollow Studs	
2	Red	3024	Plate 1 x 1	302421
1	Flat Silver	4073	Plate 1 x 1 Round	4633691
7	Red	3023	Plate 1 x 2	302321
1	Red	3794b	Plate 1 x 2 with Groove with 1 Centre Stud	379421
1	Red	92593	Plate 1 x 4 with Two Studs	4631877
2	Red	3022	Plate 2 x 2	302221, 4613974
1	Red	18674	Plate 2 x 2 Round with 1 Centre Stud	6132541
1	Black	3021	Plate 2 x 3	302126
3	Red	3021	Plate 2 x 3	302121
1	Red	3795	Plate 2 x 6	379521
1	Red	3034	Plate 2 x 8	303421
4	Red	85970	Slope Brick Curved 1 x 8 with Plate 1 x 2	4571075, 6037665, 6208565
2	Black	15068	Slope Brick Curved 2 x 2 x 0.667	6053077
2	Red	15068	Slope Brick Curved 2 x 2 x 0.667	6105976
5	Red	93273	Slope Brick Curved 4 x 1 Double	4633914
2	Black	32063	Technic Beam 6 x 0.5	4114634
2	Red	32063	Technic Beam 6 x 0.5	4118833, 4174808
2	Red	25269	Tile 1 x 1 Corner Round	6170390
3	Flat Silver	98138	Tile 1 x 1 Round with Groove	4655241
1	Black	3069b	Tile 1 x 2 with Groove	306926
1	Red	3068b	Tile 2 x 2 with Groove	306821
1	Red	26603	Tile 2 x 3	6189130
1	Red	87079	Tile 2 x 4 with Groove	4560179
1	Metallic Silver	55981	Wheel Rim 14 x 18 with Holes on Both Sides (Needs Work)	4495345, 6194811

ALIEN

As you can see in the exploded view, for the "cute monster next door," we have "misused" some parts. It's actually quite flexible because of the numerous joints. For the eye, we used a Bar 1L with Tow Ball (*BL 22484 / LEGO® 6139234*). The tongue is made from a Buffalo Horn in red (*BL 13564 / LEGO® 6160161*) and the legs are made of Elephant Trunks (*BL 43892 / LEGO® 4626202 or 6171004*).

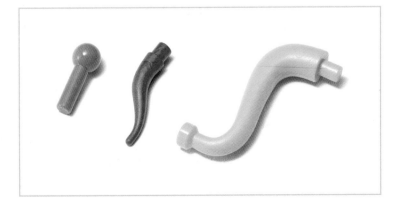

▌DISPLAY

The set can also be refined to make a display. The gray frame and the diagonally aligned plate work well to make the desert floor.

You can add some rocks or use a "Cheese Grater" (BL 61409 / LEGO® 6092115) for the cockpit ladder.

▮ CURVES

Building curves with generally square LEGO®
bricks is a bit of a challenge. However, for
longer stretches you can make use of the min-
imal leeway of accuracy of fit of LEGO® bricks
to do this. For my Dolby Theatre on Hollywood Boulevard, I used elements that were
two studs wide for each row, with one over-
lapping stud. This makes it possible to achieve
a very nice curve for the finished wall without
it becoming too unstable.

The arrows point to the studs at the base.

The archway really is just one stud deep and 40 studs wide. This allows so much leeway in the curve that, even after the bend, the fixing stud at the bottom plate can be positioned a row farther back. Thanks to the curve, the archway does not lose any width and remains 40 studs wide despite the curve.

In our example, the arch has four struts to stabilize it. Building this type of model doesn't strictly follow LEGO® guidelines of course, but it creates an unusual and eye-catching effect.

To present these ideas we selected the part of Hollywood Boulevard in Los Angeles that was also the backdrop to the movie The Italian Job (*2003*). We had a lot of fun including so many details in this 3ft-wide LEGO® scene. The Oscars are held in the Dolby Theatre every year, and it's also a popular location with tourists and tour groups looking to take photos here.

SPOCK`S EARS

You can be sure that you'll meet other vacationers on the Walk of Fame but you can't always be sure whether you're going to meet the stars themselves or their doubles. You can always stop for a photo.

You can find Spock's ears in the Batman Movies collection series (*Hair Swept Back with Pointy Light Flesh Ears Pattern, BL 93230pb04 / LEGO® 6214155*).

Rowdies!

▌GROCERY BAG

Speaking of The Italian Job: This small, behind-the-scenes scene required an idea for a grocery bag. Surprisingly, the Bucket Handle (*BL 95344 / LEGO®6245275*) can be clamped onto a log-brick quite firmly (*BL 30136 / LEGO® 4238997*).

SUPER SOAKER

You can also meet other screen heroes here. Since it is almost always hot in Los Angeles, you can have some sympathy with these little rascals here. Perhaps Spider-Man will shoot back?

TRASH CAN

A clean city needs sidewalk trash cans. At first glance, you see only what's lying next to it, not what's already in it. A Yellow Feather (*BL 4502b*) serves as a banana peel here. Inside the can, a Lipstick (*BL 93094c03 / LEGO® black 6221606*) from the Friends series is holding all the pieces together.

By the way, if you "misuse" a part, you can call it an npu (*nice part usage*).

■ HOT DOG STAND

Also typical for our scene and something we shouldn't leave out is a hot dog stand. Anyone who knows us knows that we like to work without studs. That's why we were very happy when the 2x2 Plate with Reduced Knobs (*BL 33909 / LEGO® 6212077*) appeared. Ketchup and mustard get the new round tiles with a bar as lid (*BL 20482 / LEGO® red 6215539, gold 6126113, or 6186672*). The right Bread Bun for the sausage has been available for some time now (*BL 25386 / LEGO® 6147214*).

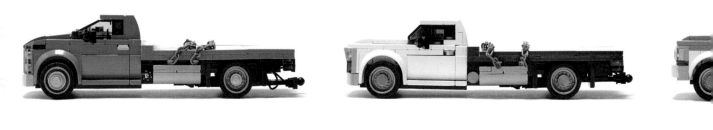
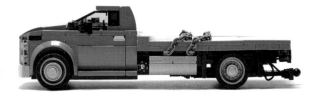

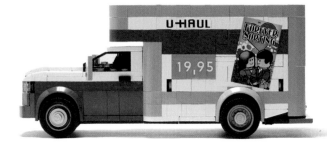

FORD F-SERIES

This project is a typical example of an occ (*our collective creation*). The first draft was an ambulance created by our friend Eugen Sellin. Uwe and I developed it over a few months and came up with something special for this set of instructions.

■ FORD F-SERIES CHASSIS

Now decide for yourself which version of a Ford F-Series model you'd like to build. Here is just the basic chassis. Building on this, you can then decide if you want to build an older or a modern version.

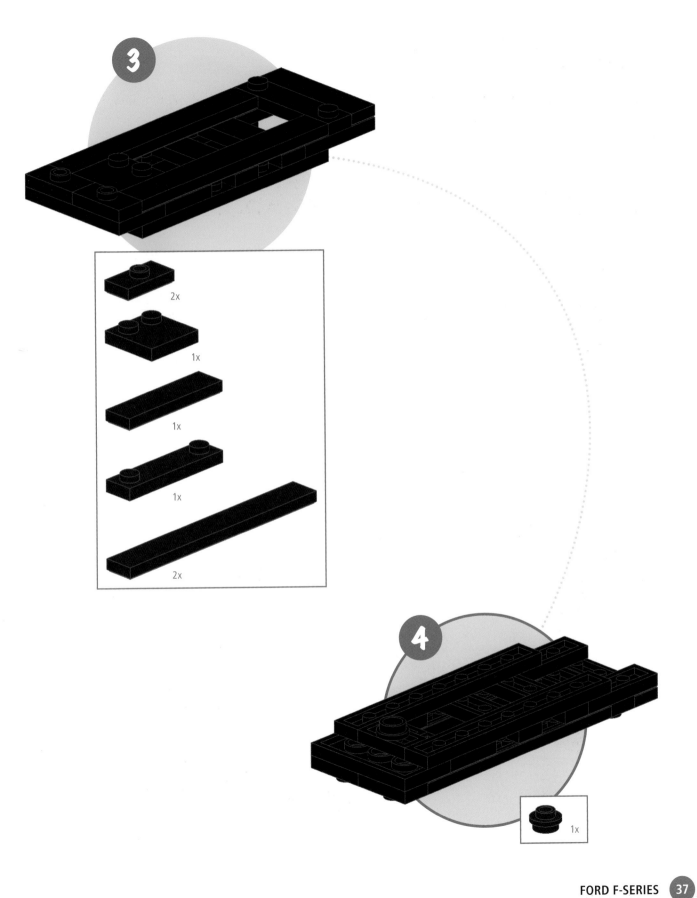

3

2x

1x

1x

1x

2x

4

1x

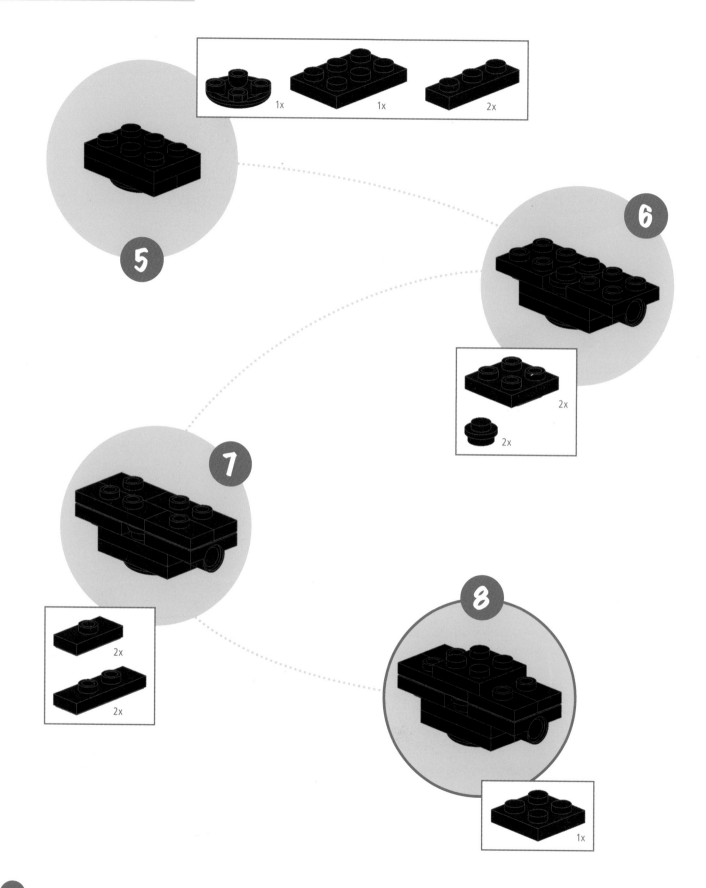

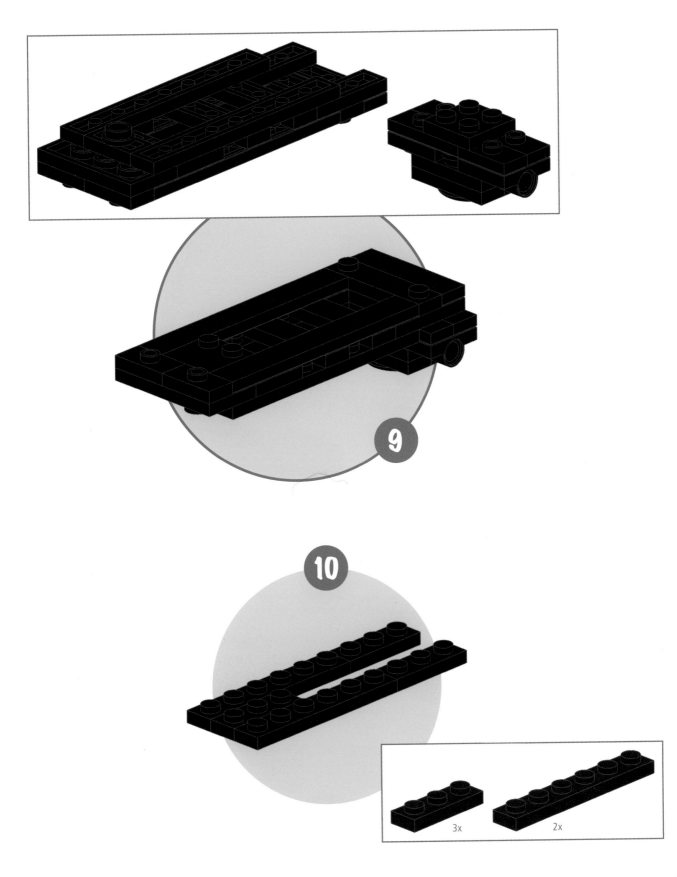

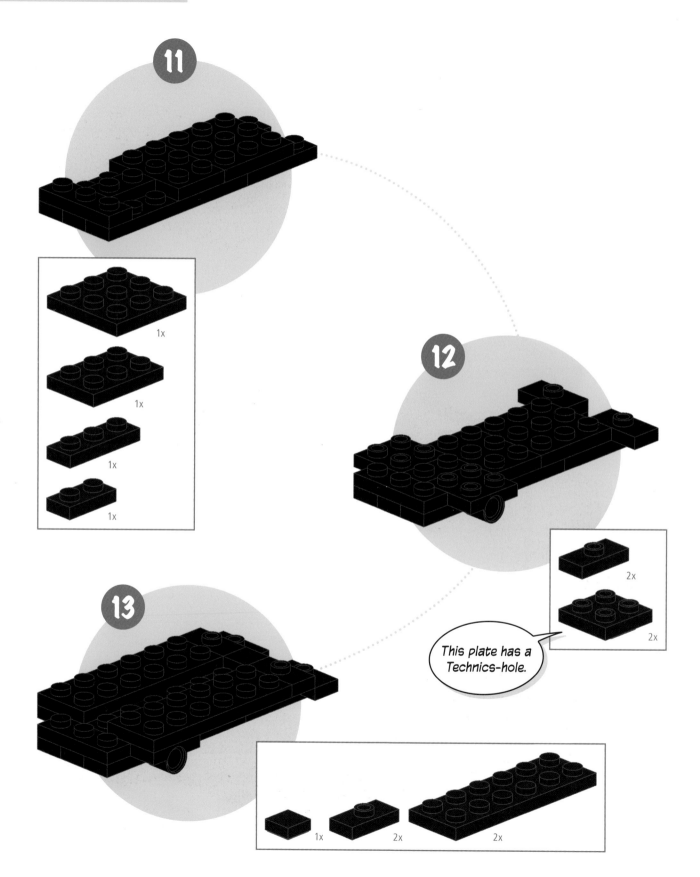

This plate has a Technics-hole.

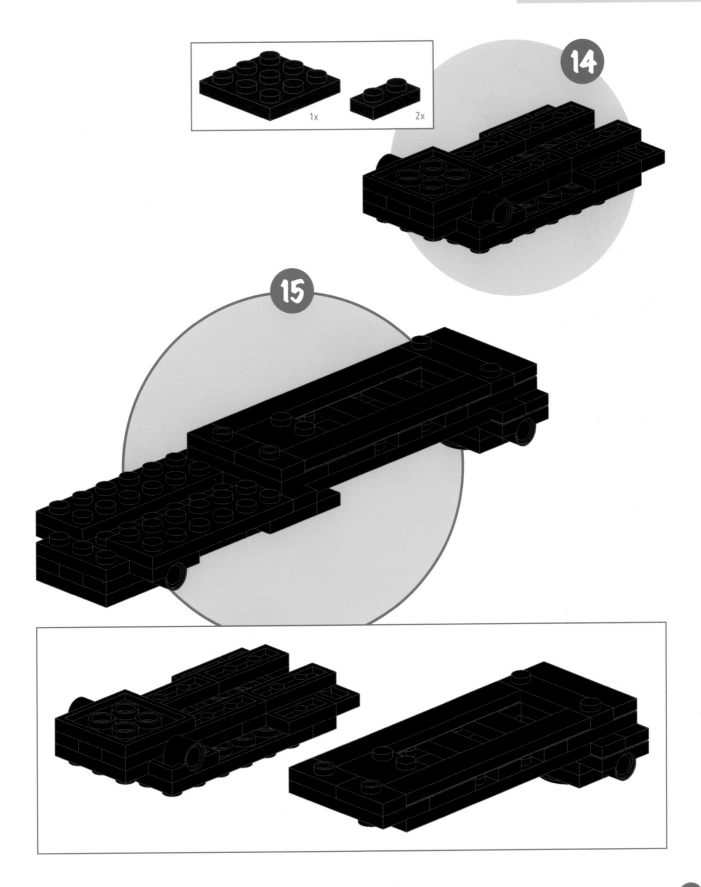

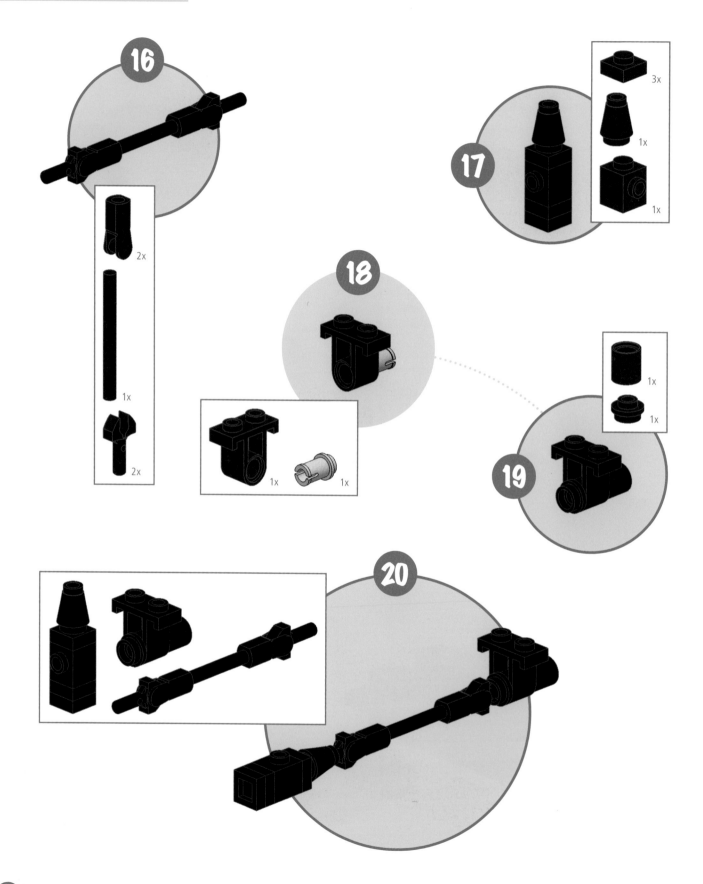

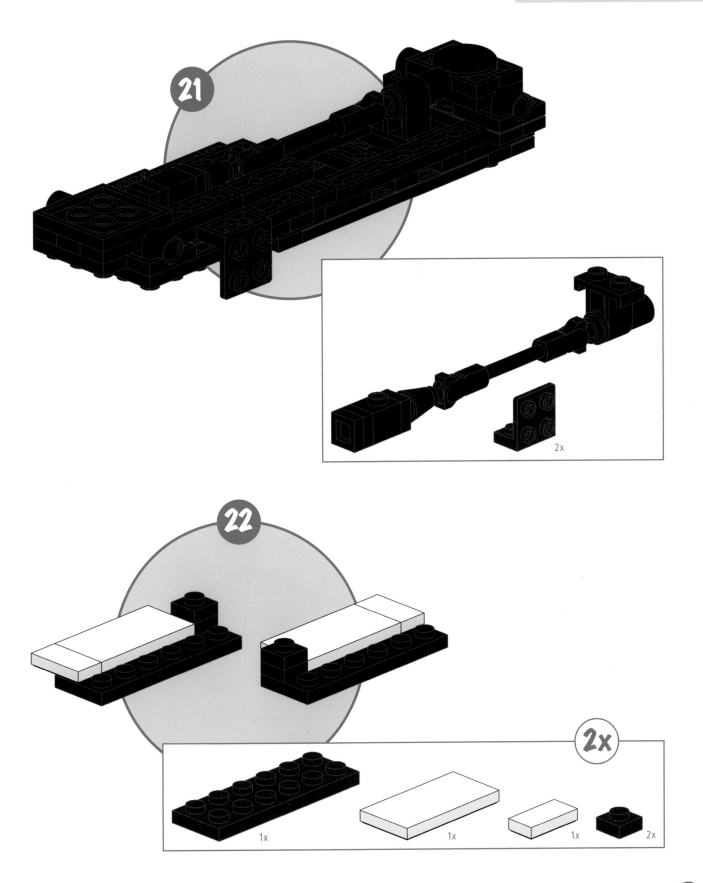

21

2x

22

2x

1x

1x

1x

2x

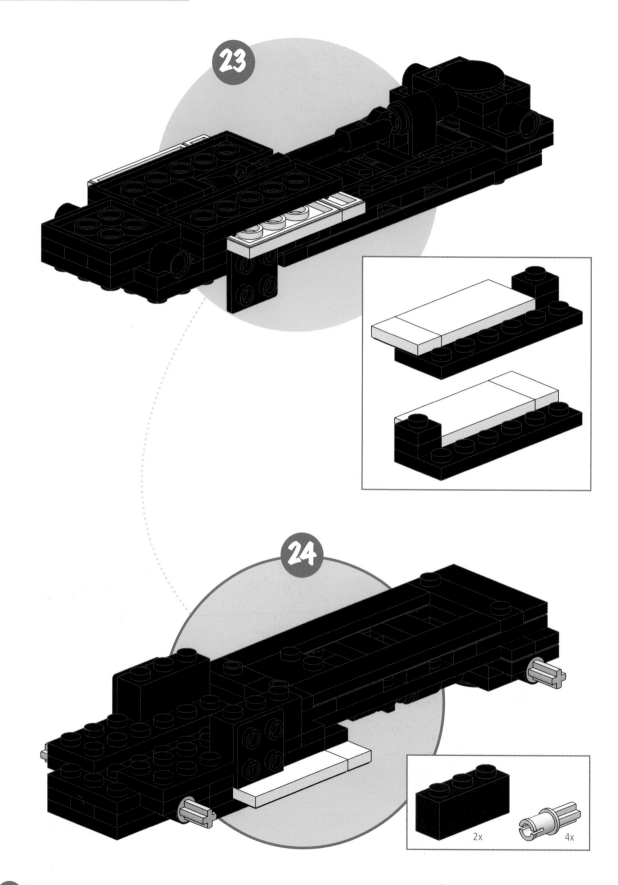

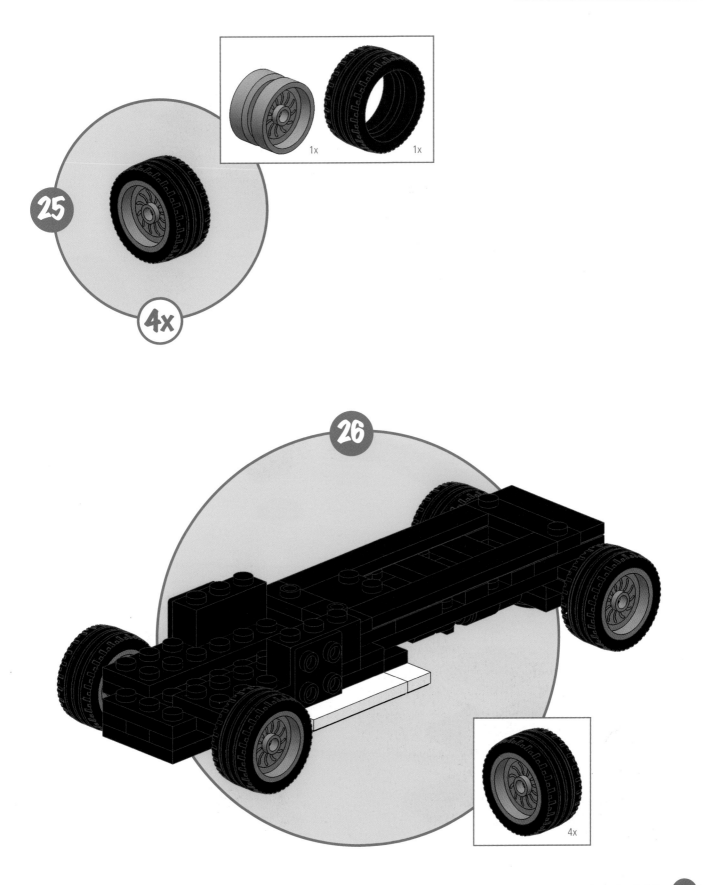

PARTS LIST

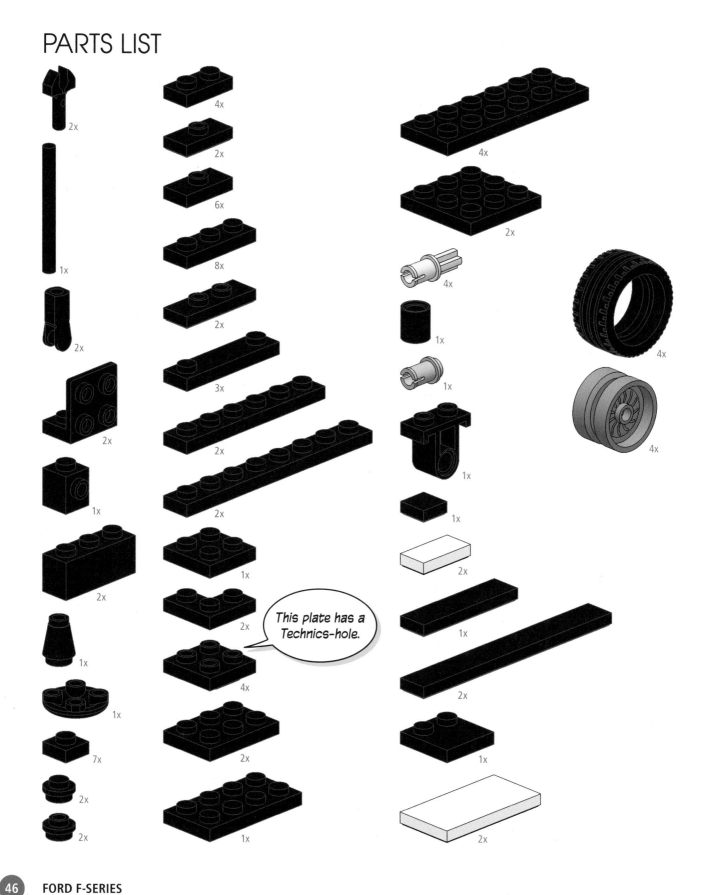

This plate has a Technics-hole.

Amount	Color		Part number	Name	LEGO® Part number
2		Black	48729b	Bar 1.5L with Clip with Truncated Sides and Hole in Shaft	4289538
1		Black	30374	Bar 4L Lightsaber Blade	3037426, 4140303, 6116604
2		Black	23443	Bar Tube with Handle	6143318
2		Black	99207	Bracket 1 x 2 - 2 x 2 Up	6000650
1		Black	87087	Brick 1 x 1 with Stud on 1 Side	4558954
2		Black	3622	Brick 1 x 3	362226
1		Black	4589b	Cone 1 x 1 with Stop	4518219, 4529236, 458926
1		Black	2654	Dish 2 x 2	265426, 4278359, 4617551
7		Black	3024	Plate 1 x 1	302426
2		Black	4073	Plate 1 x 1 Round	614126
2		Black	85861	Plate 1 x 1 Round with Open Stud	6100627, 6168646
4		Black	3023	Plate 1 x 2	302326
2		Black	15573	Plate 1 x 2 with Groove with 1 Centre Stud, without Understud	6092585
6		Black	3794a	Plate 1 x 2 without Groove with 1 Centre Stud	379426
8		Black	3623	Plate 1 x 3	362326
2		Black	34103	Plate 1 x 3 with 2 Studs Offset	6199908
3		Black	92593	Plate 1 x 4 with Two Studs	4599499
2		Black	3666	Plate 1 x 6	366626
2		Black	3460	Plate 1 x 8	346026
1		Black	3022	Plate 2 x 2	302226
2		Black	2420	Plate 2 x 2 Corner	242026
4		Black	10247	Plate 2 x 2 with Hole and Complete Underside Rib	6061032
2		Black	3021	Plate 2 x 3	302126
1		Black	3020	Plate 2 x 4	302026
4		Black	3795	Plate 2 x 6	379526
2		Black	11212	Plate 3 x 3	6174917
4		Tan	3749	Technic Axle Pin	4186017, 4666579, 65625
1		Black	18654	Technic Beam 1	6121485
1		Light Bluish Gray	4274	Technic Pin 1/2	4211483, 4274194
1		Black	32529	Technic Pin Joiner Plate 1 x 2 x 1 & 1/2	4144023
1		Black	3070b	Tile 1 x 1 with Groove	307026
2		White	3069b	Tile 1 x 2 with Groove	306901
1		Black	2431	Tile 1 x 4 with Groove	243126
2		Black	4162	Tile 1 x 8	416226
1		Black	33909	Tile 2 x 2 with Studs on Edge	6192346
2		White	87079	Tile 2 x 4 with Groove	4560178
4		Black	18977	Tyre 11.2/ 28 x 17.6 Intermediate	6102596
4		Flat Silver	18976	Wheel Rim 11 x 18 with Vented Disc Brake	6102594

1978 FORD F-SERIES

Here are the instructions for the 1978 version of the Ford F-150. If you would rather build a 2015 version, go to page 59.

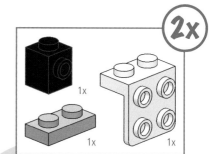

1

1x
1x   2x

2x

2x

1x
1x   1x

2

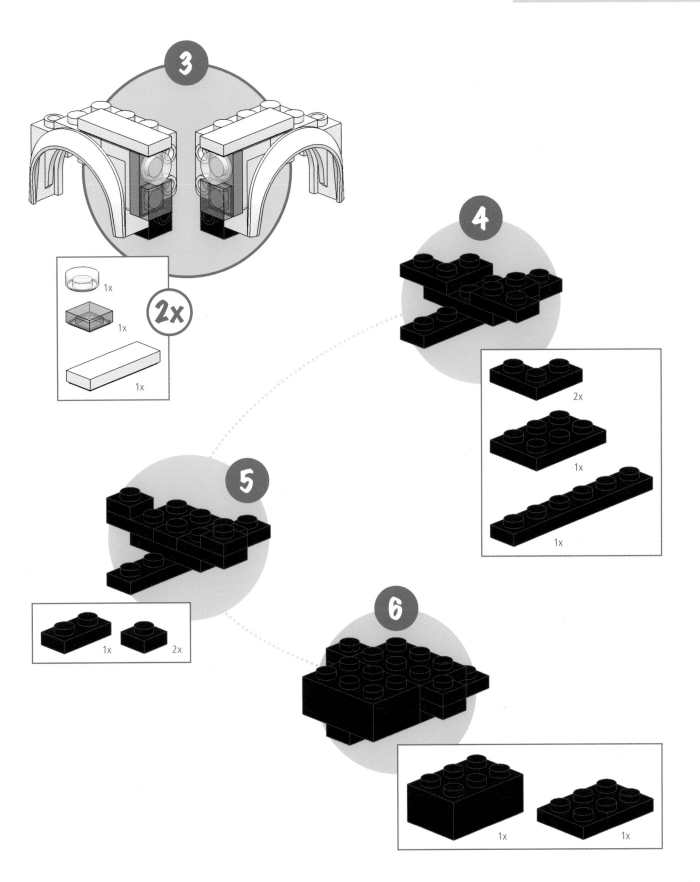

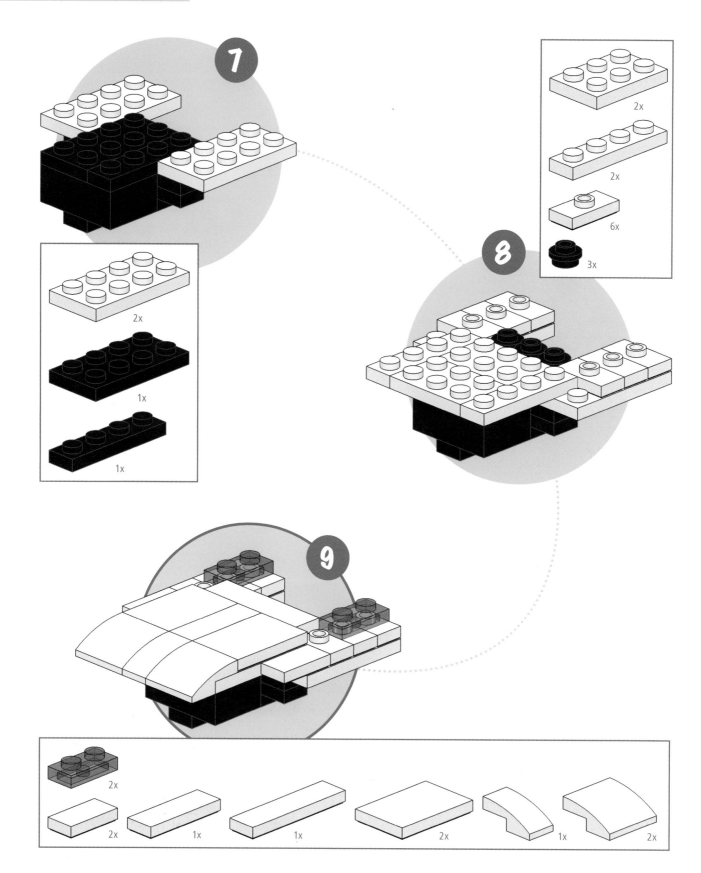

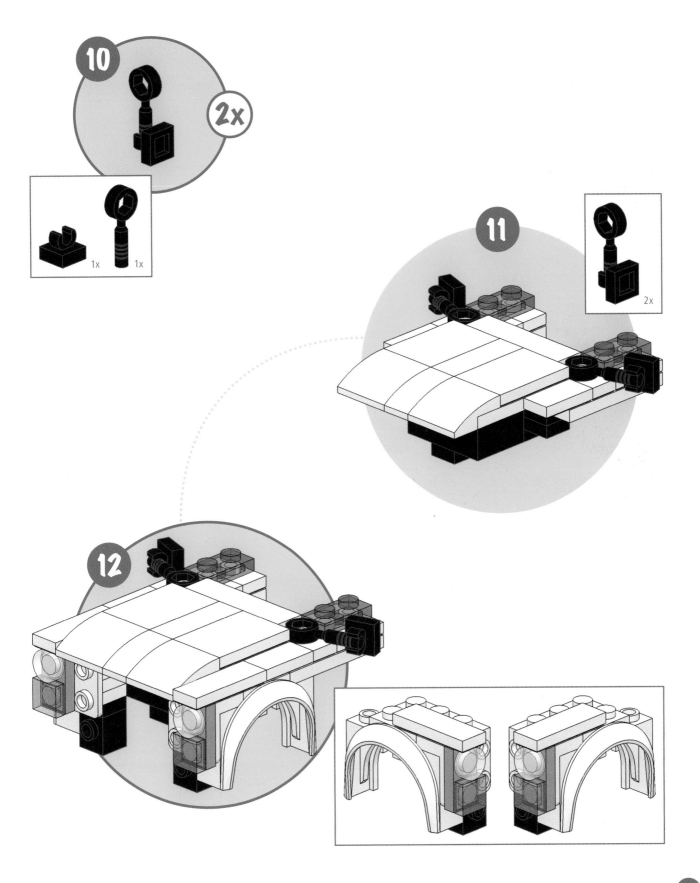

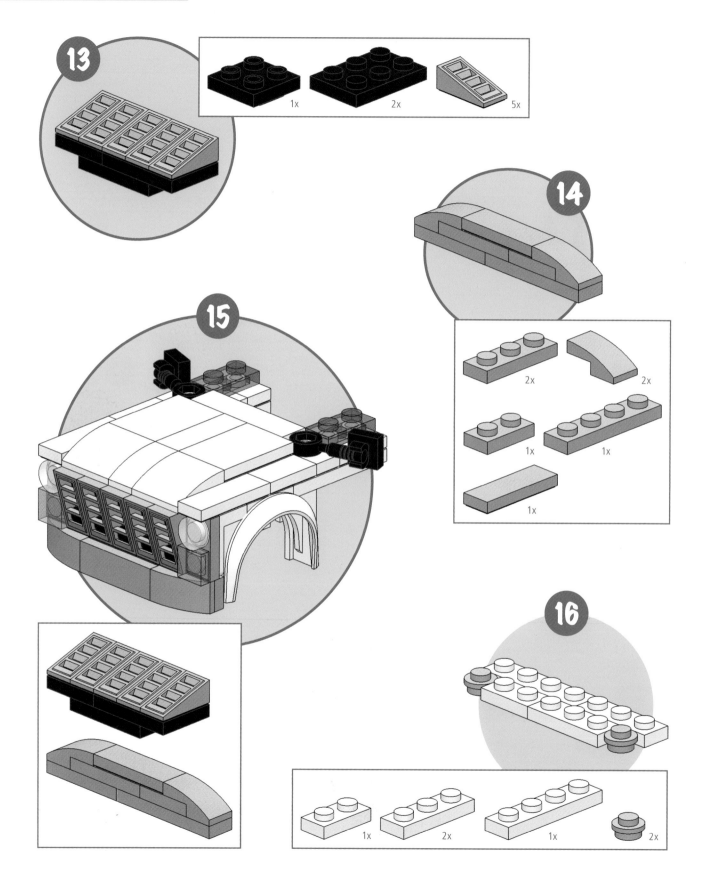

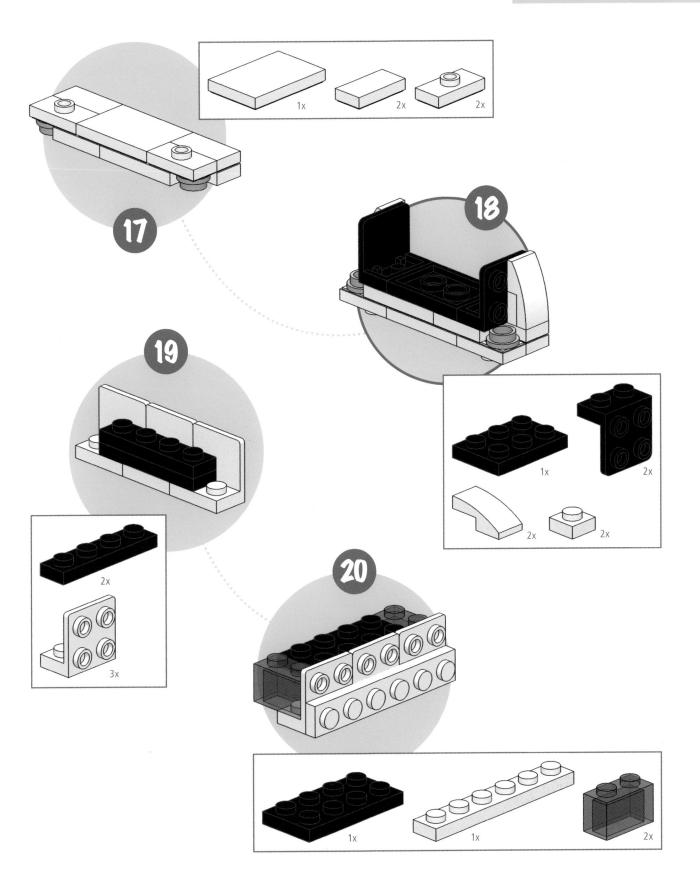

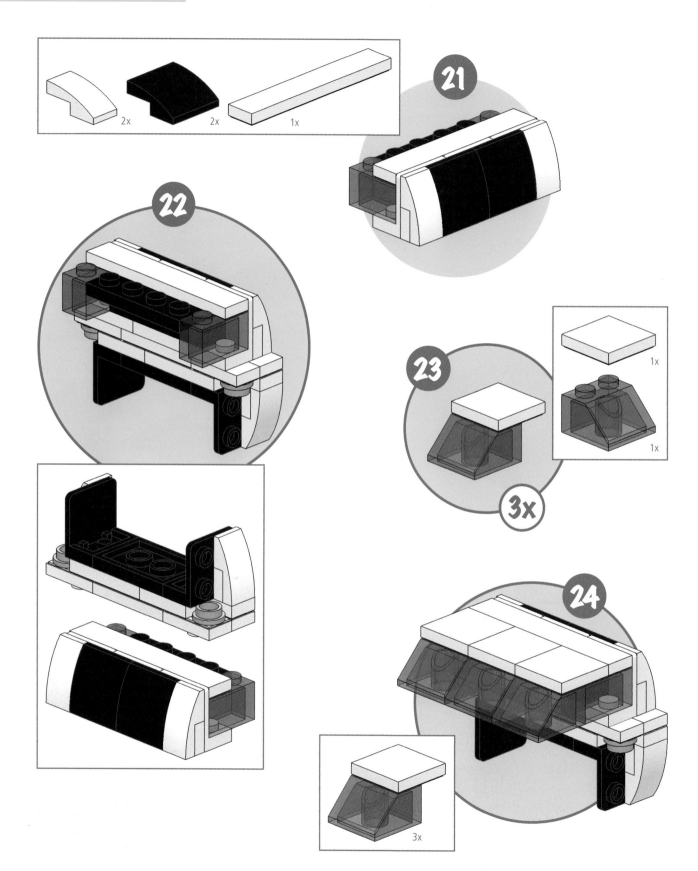

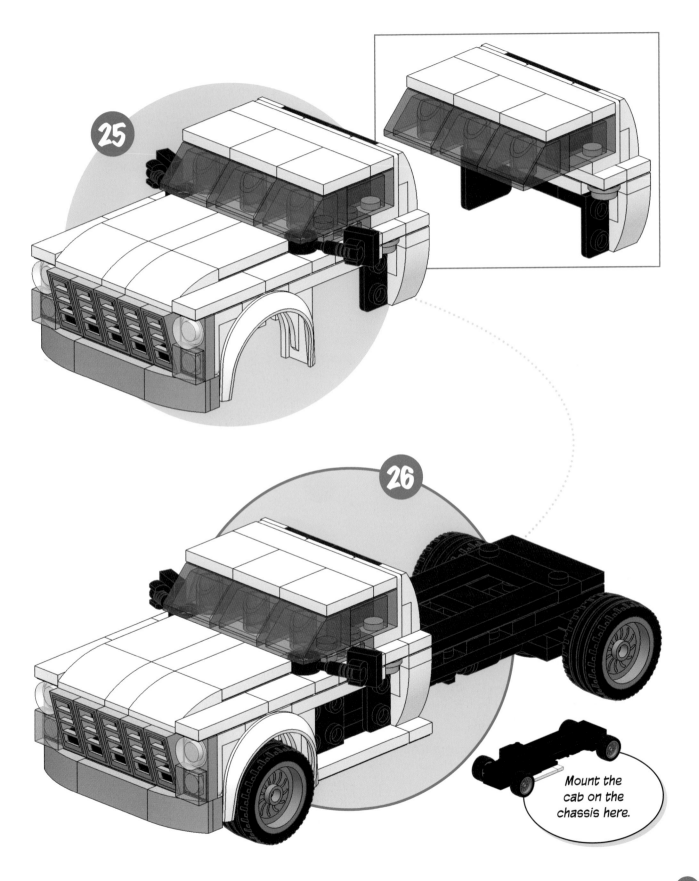

Mount the cab on the chassis here.

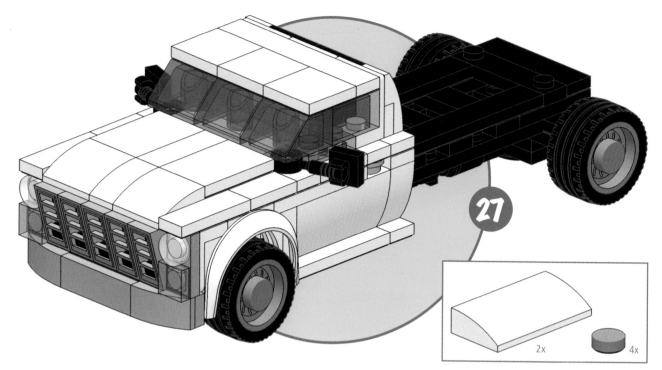

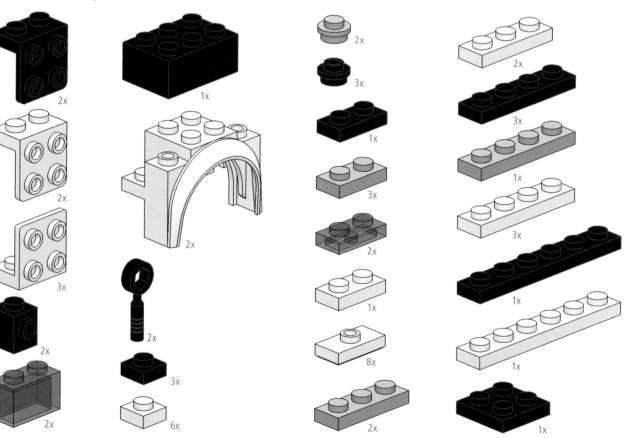

PARTS LIST

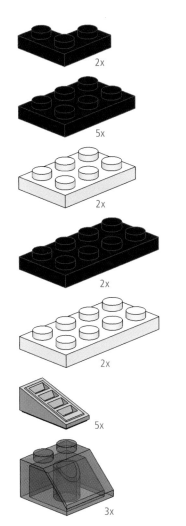

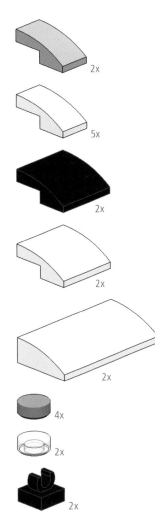

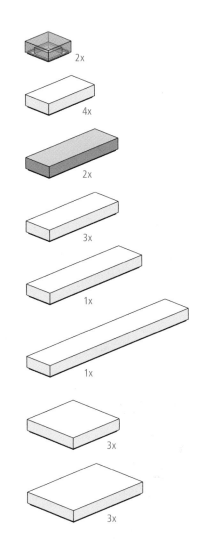

Amount	Color		Part number	Name	LEGO® Part number
2	⬛	Black	44728	Bracket 1 x 2 - 2 x 2	4184645, 4277932, 6048855, 6117973
2		White	44728	Bracket 1 x 2 - 2 x 2	4203147, 4277926, 4615649, 6117940
3		White	99207	Bracket 1 x 2 - 2 x 2 Up	6097637
2	⬛	Black	87087	Brick 1 x 1 with Stud on 1 Side	4558954
2		Trans Black	3065	Brick 1 x 2 without Centre Stud	3065111, 4226179, 6244909
1	⬛	Black	3002	Brick 2 x 3	300226
2		White	18974	Car Mudguard 4 x 2.5 x 2.333	6102583
2	⬛	Black	604552	Minifig Tool Box Wrench with 3-Rib Handle	6030875
3	⬛	Black	3024	Plate 1 x 1	302426
6		White	3024	Plate 1 x 1	302401
2		Metallic Silver	4073	Plate 1 x 1 Round	4249039, 51809301, 6051507
3	⬛	Black	85861	Plate 1 x 1 Round with Open Stud	6100627, 6168646

Amount	Color	Part number	Name	LEGO® Part number
1	Black	3023	Plate 1 x 2	302326
3	Light Bluish Gray	3023	Plate 1 x 2	3023194, 4211398
2	Trans Black	3023	Plate 1 x 2	6001197, 6240219
1	White	3023	Plate 1 x 2	302301
8	White	15573	Plate 1 x 2 with Groove with 1 Centre Stud, without Understud	379401, 6051511
2	Light Bluish Gray	3623	Plate 1 x 3	3623194, 4211429
2	White	3623	Plate 1 x 3	362301
3	Black	3710	Plate 1 x 4	371026
1	Light Bluish Gray	3710	Plate 1 x 4	4211445
3	White	3710	Plate 1 x 4	371001
1	Black	3666	Plate 1 x 6	366626
1	White	3666	Plate 1 x 6	366601
1	Black	3022	Plate 2 x 2	302226
2	Black	2420	Plate 2 x 2 Corner	242026
5	Black	3021	Plate 2 x 3	302126
2	White	3021	Plate 2 x 3	302101
2	Black	3020	Plate 2 x 4	302026
2	White	3020	Plate 2 x 4	302001
5	Light Bluish Gray	61409	Slope Brick 18 2 x 1 x 0.667 Grille	6092111
3	Trans Black	3039	Slope Brick 45 2 x 2	4164276, 6227111
2	Light Bluish Gray	11477	Slope Brick Curved 2 x 1	6028813
5	White	11477	Slope Brick Curved 2 x 1	6034044
2	Black	15068	Slope Brick Curved 2 x 2 x 0.667	6053077
2	White	15068	Slope Brick Curved 2 x 2 x 0.667	6047220
2	White	88930	Slope Brick Curved 2 x 4 with Underside Studs	4583297
4	Flat Silver	98138	Tile 1 x 1 Round with Groove	4655241
2	Trans Clear	98138	Tile 1 x 1 Round with Groove	4650498
2	Black	15712	Tile 1 x 1 with Clip (Thick C-Clip)	6066102
2	Trans Orange	3070b	Tile 1 x 1 with Groove	6109457
4	White	3069b	Tile 1 x 2 with Groove	306901
1	Light Bluish Gray	63864	Tile 1 x 3 with Groove	4558169
3	White	63864	Tile 1 x 3 with Groove	4558168
1	White	2431	Tile 1 x 4 with Groove	243101
1	White	6636	Tile 1 x 6	663601
3	White	3068b	Tile 2 x 2 with Groove	306801
3	White	26603	Tile 2 x 3	6156667

2015 FORD F-SERIES

This 2015 version of the F-150 is clearly much more modern.

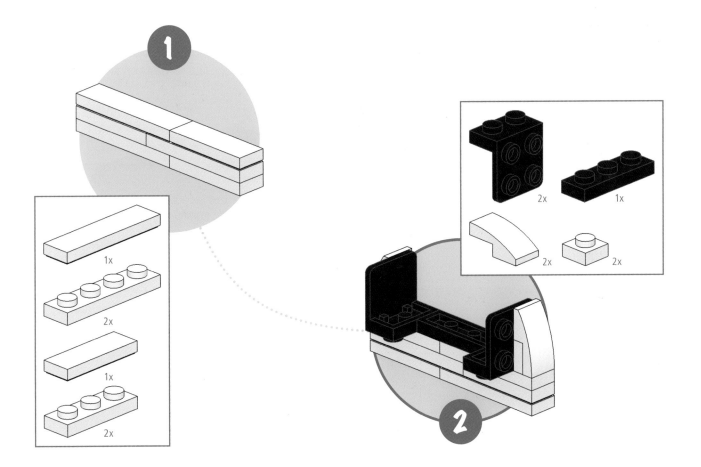

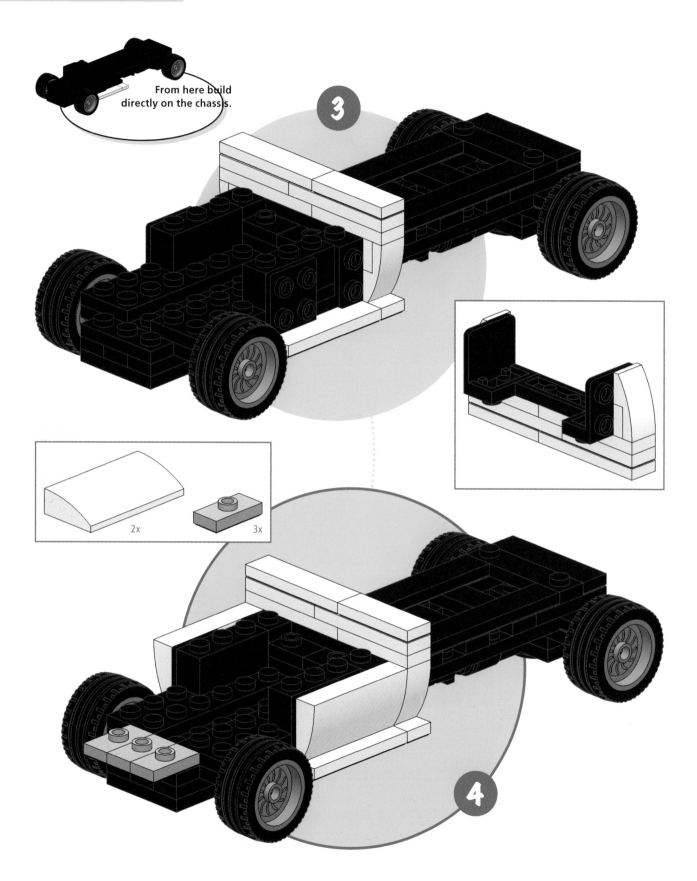

From here build directly on the chassis.

2x   3x

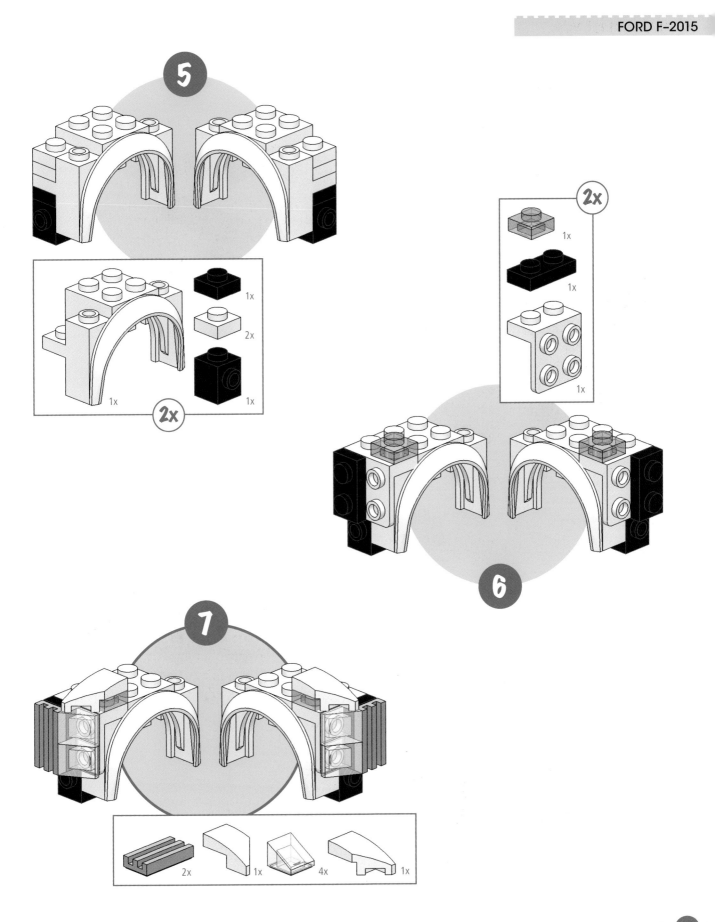

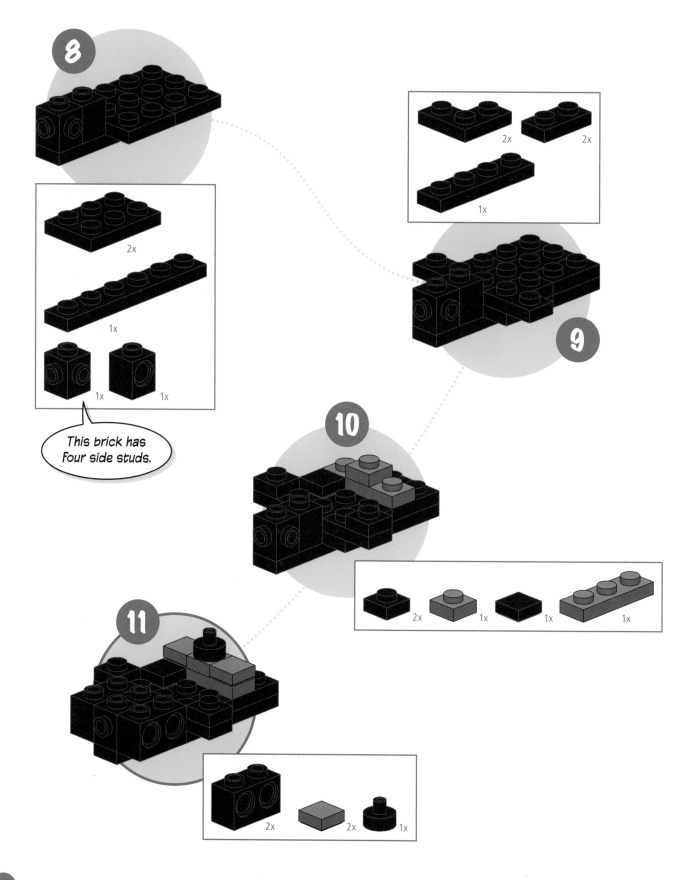

This brick has
four side studs.

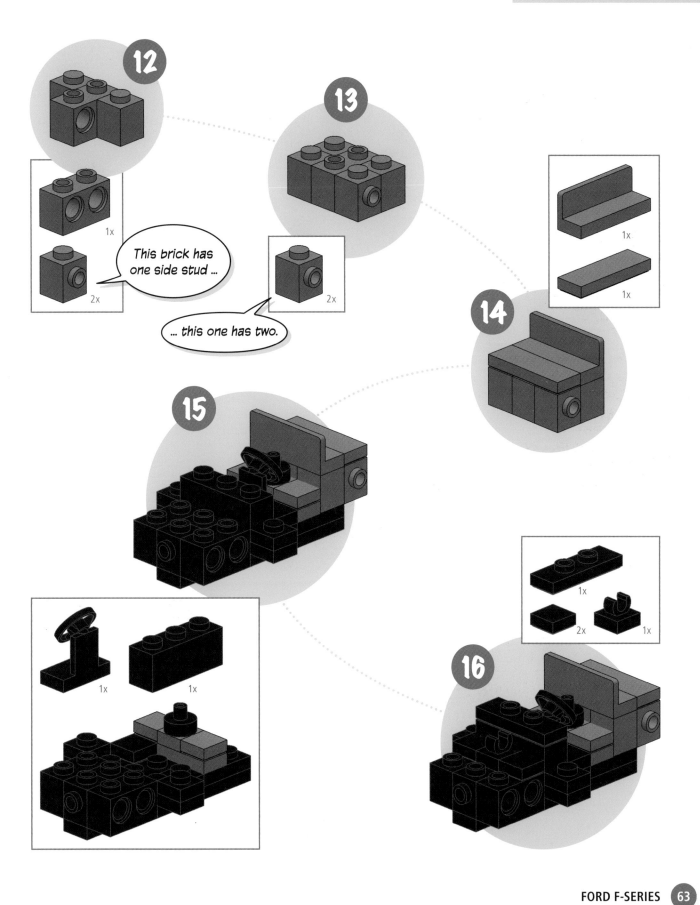

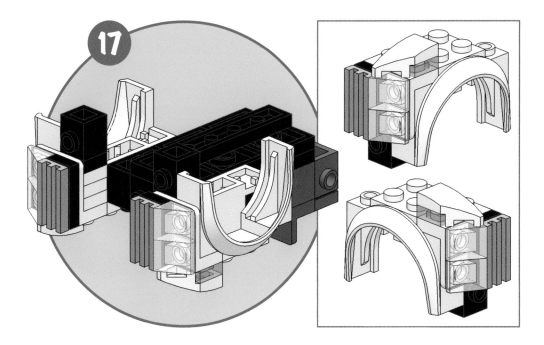

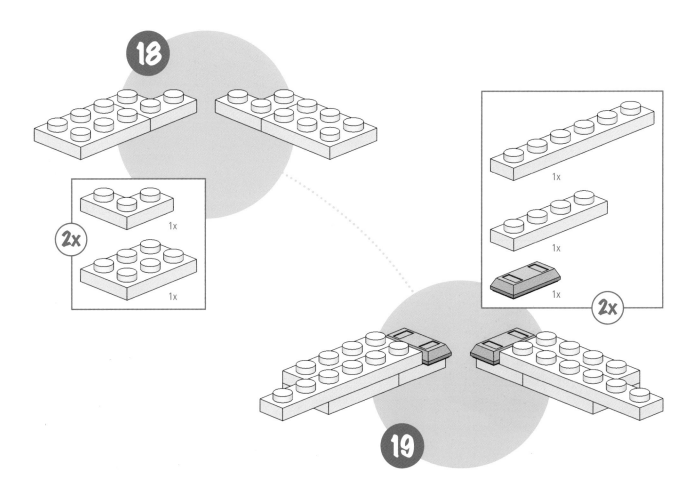

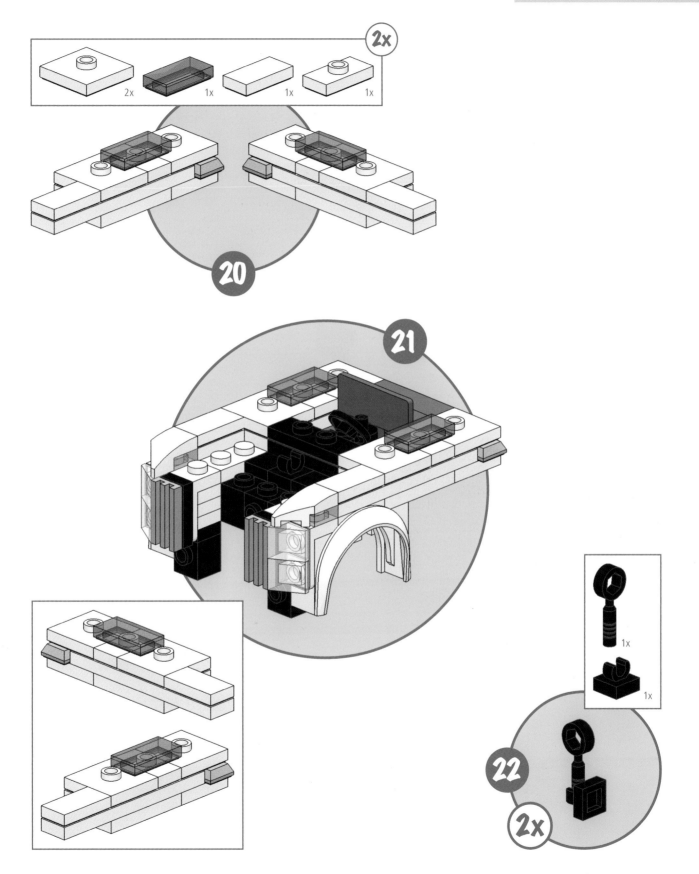

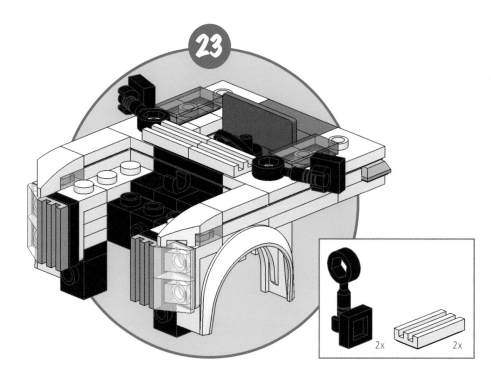

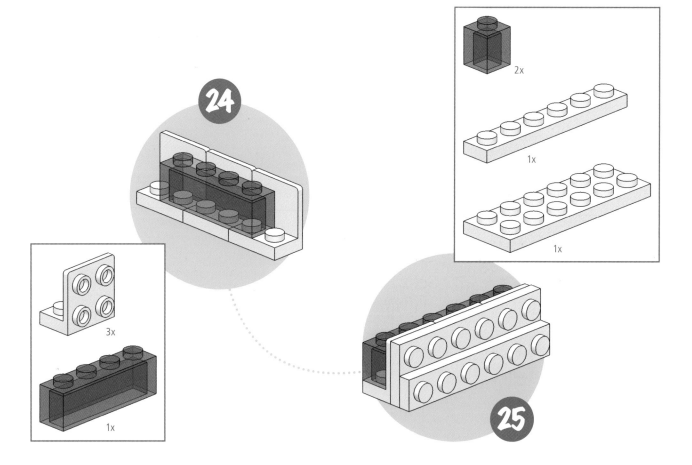

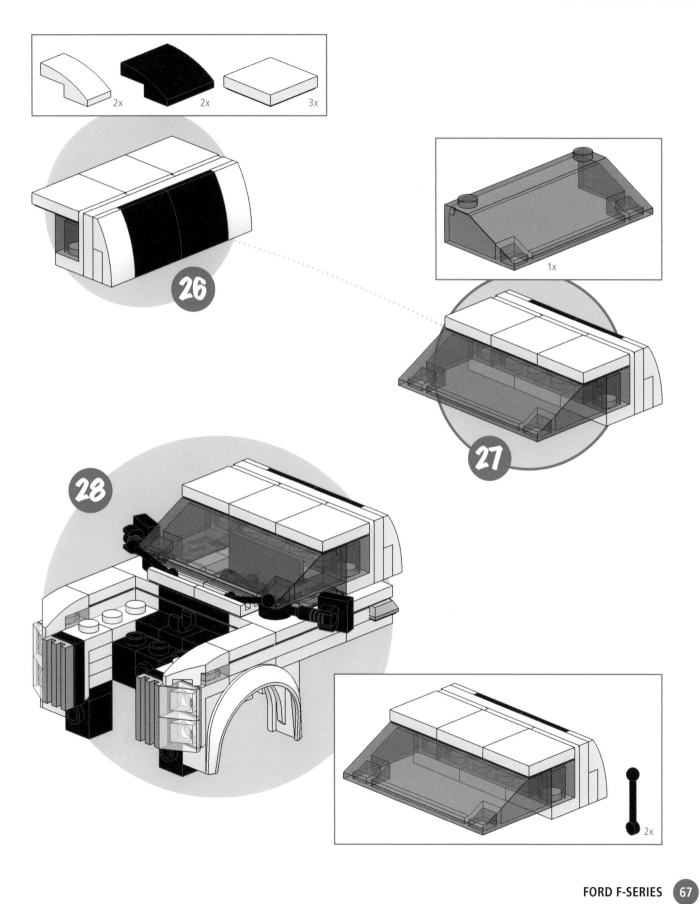

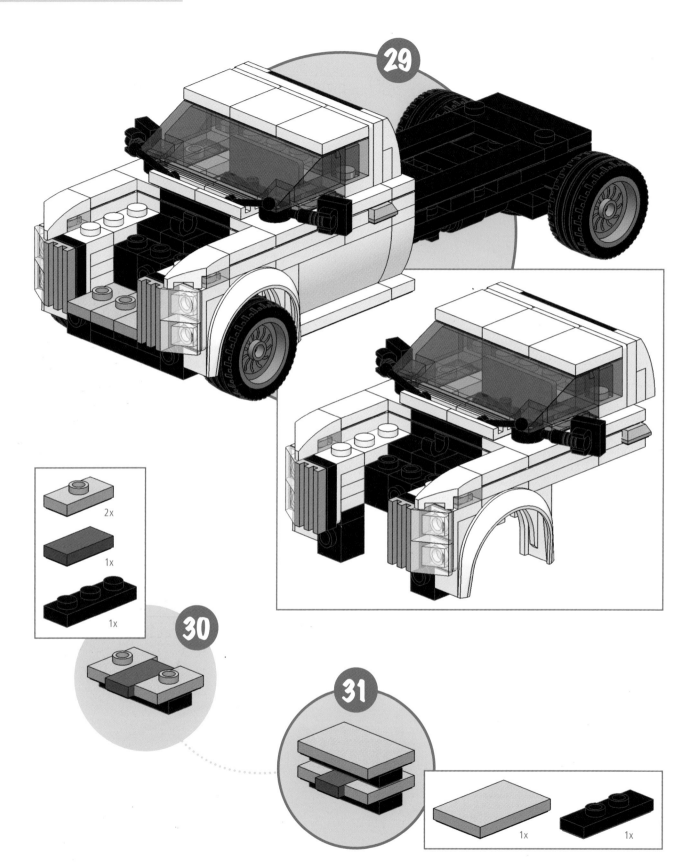

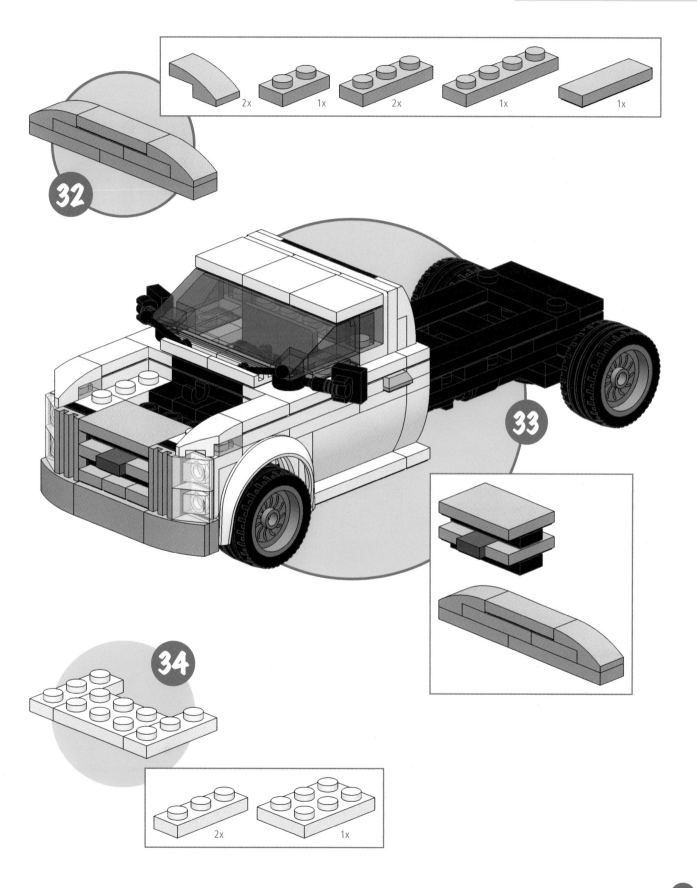

32

33

34

2x 1x 2x 1x 1x

2x 1x

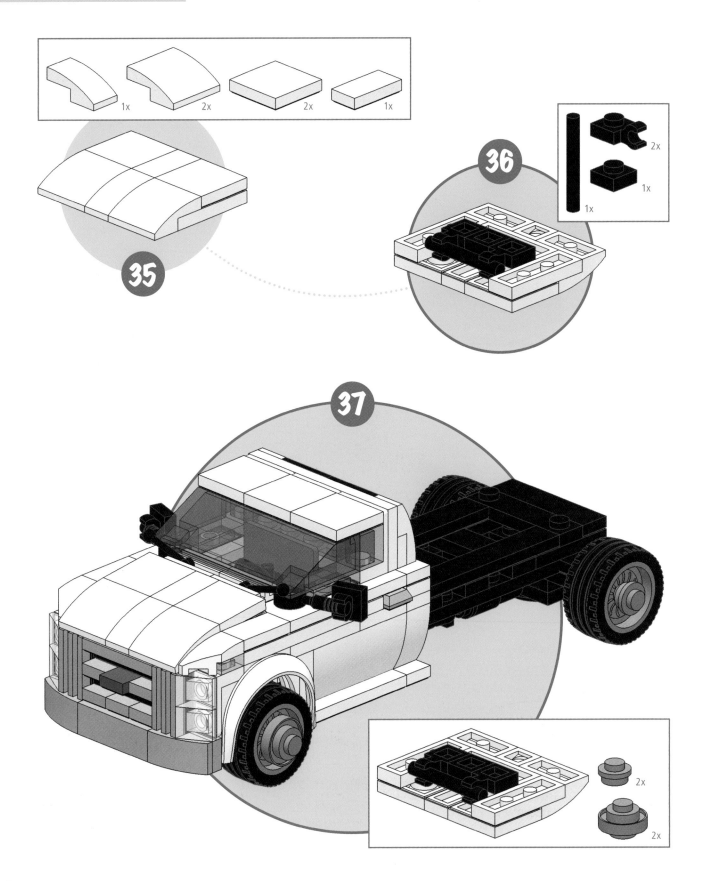

PARTS LIST

1x

2x

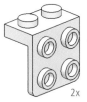

2x

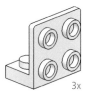

3x

2x

2x

2x

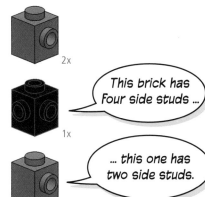

This brick has four side studs ...

1x

... this one has two side studs.

2x

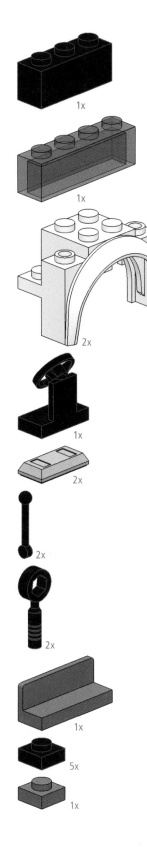

1x

1x

2x

2x

1x

5x

1x

2x

2x

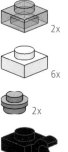

2x

6x

2x

2x

4x

1x

5x

2x

2x

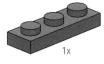

1x

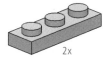

2x

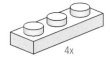

4x

2x

1x

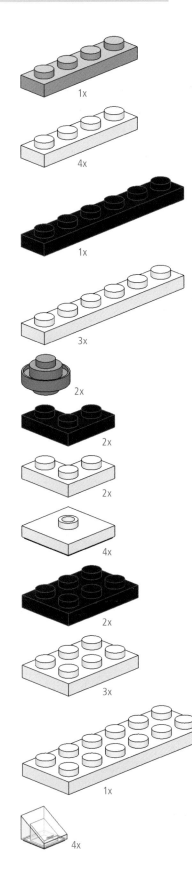

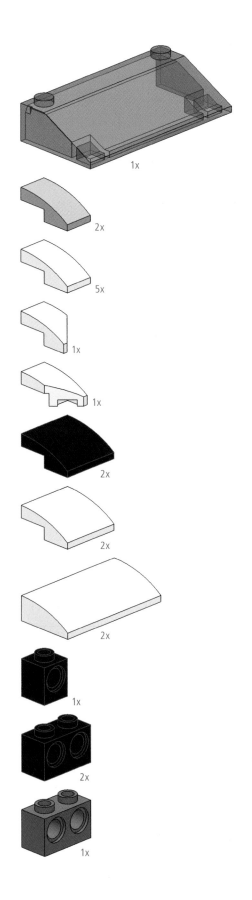

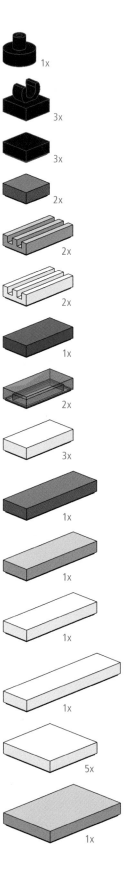

Amount	Color	Part number	Name	LEGO® Part number
1	Black	87994	Bar 3L	4566275, 4653208, 6093525
2	Black	44728	Bracket 1 x 2 - 2 x 2	4184645, 4277932, 6048855, 6117973
2	White	44728	Bracket 1 x 2 - 2 x 2	4203147, 4277926, 4615649, 6117940
3	White	99207	Bracket 1 x 2 - 2 x 2 Up	6097637
2	Trans Black	3005	Brick 1 x 1	6102359, 6240554
2	Black	87087	Brick 1 x 1 with Stud on 1 Side	4558954
2	Dark Bluish Gray	87087	Brick 1 x 1 with Stud on 1 Side	4558955
1	Black	4733	Brick 1 x 1 with Studs on Four Sides	473326
2	Dark Bluish Gray	47905	Brick 1 x 1 with Studs on Two Opposite Sides	4213574
1	Black	3622	Brick 1 x 3	362226
1	Trans Black	3066	Brick 1 x 4 without Centre Studs	4198311, 6245290
2	White	18974	Car Mudguard 4 x 2.5 x 2.333	6102583
1	Black	3829c01	Car Steering Stand and Wheel (Complete)	73081
2	Light Bluish Gray	99563	Gold Ingot	6134378
2	Black	4593	Hinge Control Stick	
2	Black	11402i	Minifig Tool Box Wrench with 3-Rib Handle	6030875
1	Dark Bluish Gray	23950	Panel 1 x 3 x 1 with Rounded Corners	6149768
5	Black	3024	Plate 1 x 1	302426
1	Dark Bluish Gray	3024	Plate 1 x 1	4210719
2	Trans Orange	3024	Plate 1 x 1	4542673, 6252040
6	White	3024	Plate 1 x 1	302401
2	Flat Silver	4073	Plate 1 x 1 Round	4633691
2	Black	4085d	Plate 1 x 1 with Clip Horizontal (Thick C-Clip)	4550017, 4617547
4	Black	3023	Plate 1 x 2	302326
1	Light Bluish Gray	3023	Plate 1 x 2	3023194, 4211398
5	Light Bluish Gray	15573	Plate 1 x 2 with Groove with 1 Centre Stud, without Understud	6066097
2	White	15573	Plate 1 x 2 with Groove with 1 Centre Stud, without Understud	379401, 6051511
2	Black	3623	Plate 1 x 3	362326
1	Dark Bluish Gray	3623	Plate 1 x 3	4211133
2	Light Bluish Gray	3623	Plate 1 x 3	3623194, 4211429
4	White	3623	Plate 1 x 3	362301
2	Black	34103	Plate 1 x 3 with 2 Studs Offset	6199908
1	Black	3710	Plate 1 x 4	371026
1	Light Bluish Gray	3710	Plate 1 x 4	4211445
4	White	3710	Plate 1 x 4	371001
1	Black	3666	Plate 1 x 6	366626

Amount		Color	Part number	Name	LEGO® Part number
3		White	3666	Plate 1 x 6	366601
2		Flat Silver	91049	Plate 1.5 x 1.5 x 0.667 Round	6092258
2		Black	2420	Plate 2 x 2 Corner	242026
2		White	2420	Plate 2 x 2 Corner	242001
4		White	87580	Plate 2 x 2 with Groove with 1 Centre Stud	4565324, 6126046
2		Black	3021	Plate 2 x 3	302126
3		White	3021	Plate 2 x 3	302101
1		White	3795	Plate 2 x 6	379501
4		Trans Clear	54200	Slope Brick 31 1 x 1 x 0.667	4244362, 6245250
1		Trans Black	58181	Slope Brick 33 3 x 6 without Inner Walls	4498370, 6230116
2		Light Bluish Gray	11477	Slope Brick Curved 2 x 1	6028813
5		White	11477	Slope Brick Curved 2 x 1	6034044
1		White	29120	Slope Brick Curved 2 x 1 with Cutout Left	6213880
1		White	29119	Slope Brick Curved 2 x 1 with Cutout Right	6213881
2		Black	15068	Slope Brick Curved 2 x 2 x 0.667	6053077
2		White	15068	Slope Brick Curved 2 x 2 x 0.667	6047220
2		White	88930	Slope Brick Curved 2 x 4 with Underside Studs	4583297
1		Black	6541	Technic Brick 1 x 1 with Hole	654126
2		Black	32000	Technic Brick 1 x 2 with Holes	3200026
1		Dark Bluish Gray	32000	Technic Brick 1 x 2 with Holes	4210762
1		Black	20482	Tile 1 x 1 Round with Pin and Pin Hole	6167933, 6186675
2		Black	15712	Tile 1 x 1 with Clip (Thick C-Clip)	6066102
3		Black	3070b	Tile 1 x 1 with Groove	307026
2		Dark Bluish Gray	3070b	Tile 1 x 1 with Groove	4210848
2		Light Bluish Gray	2412b	Tile 1 x 2 Grille with Groove	4211350
2		White	2412b	Tile 1 x 2 Grille with Groove	241201
1		Blue	3069b	Tile 1 x 2 with Groove	306923
2		Trans Black	3069b	Tile 1 x 2 with Groove	4250471, 4529685, 6251292
3		White	3069b	Tile 1 x 2 with Groove	306901
1		Dark Bluish Gray	63864	Tile 1 x 3 with Groove	4568734
1		Light Bluish Gray	63864	Tile 1 x 3 with Groove	4558169
1		White	63864	Tile 1 x 3 with Groove	4558168
1		White	2431	Tile 1 x 4 with Groove	243101
5		White	3068b	Tile 2 x 2 with Groove	306801
1		Light Bluish Gray	26603	Tile 2 x 3	6171894

FORD F-SERIES FLATBED CONSTRUCTION

We've designed the car so you can create different builds of your own choice. As a uniform first-level version, here is the flatbed with simple, unprinted tiles. We really take off on the opening double-page spread.

1

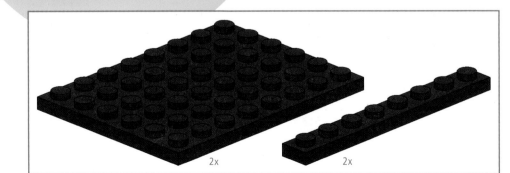

2x   2x

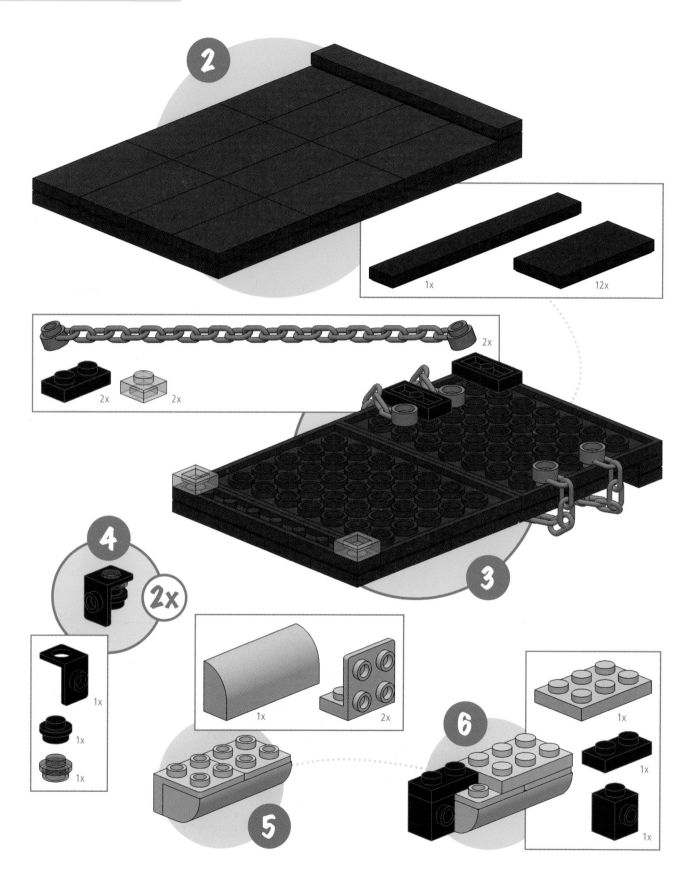

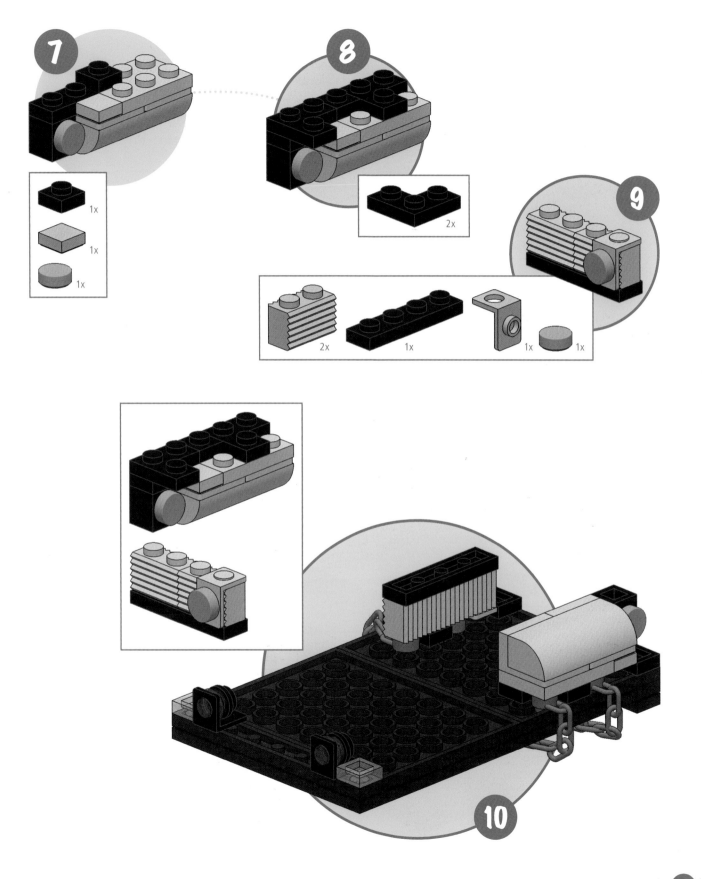

7

1x
1x
1x

8

2x

9

2x   1x   1x   1x

10

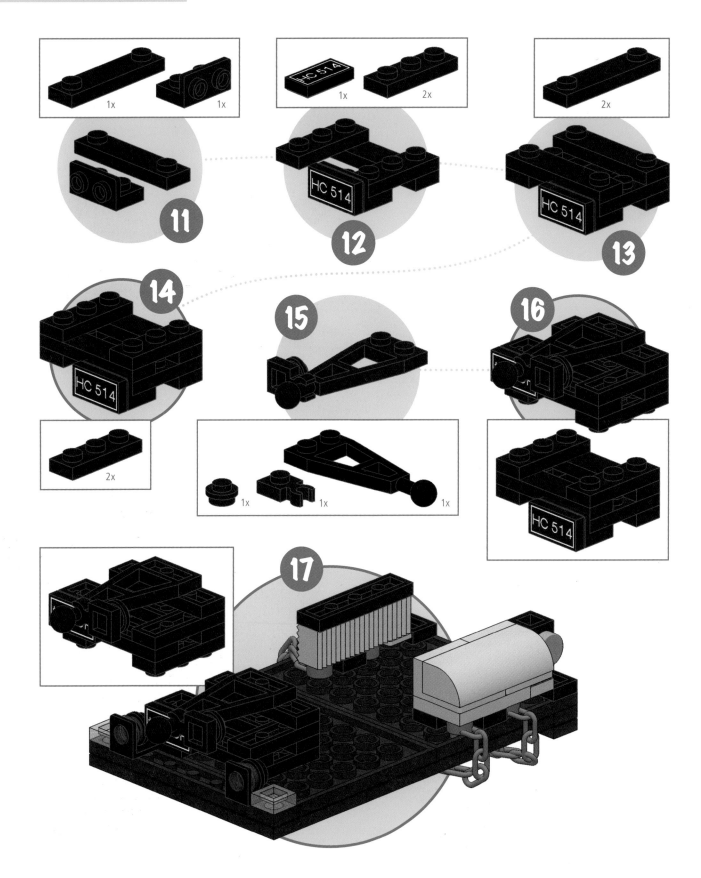

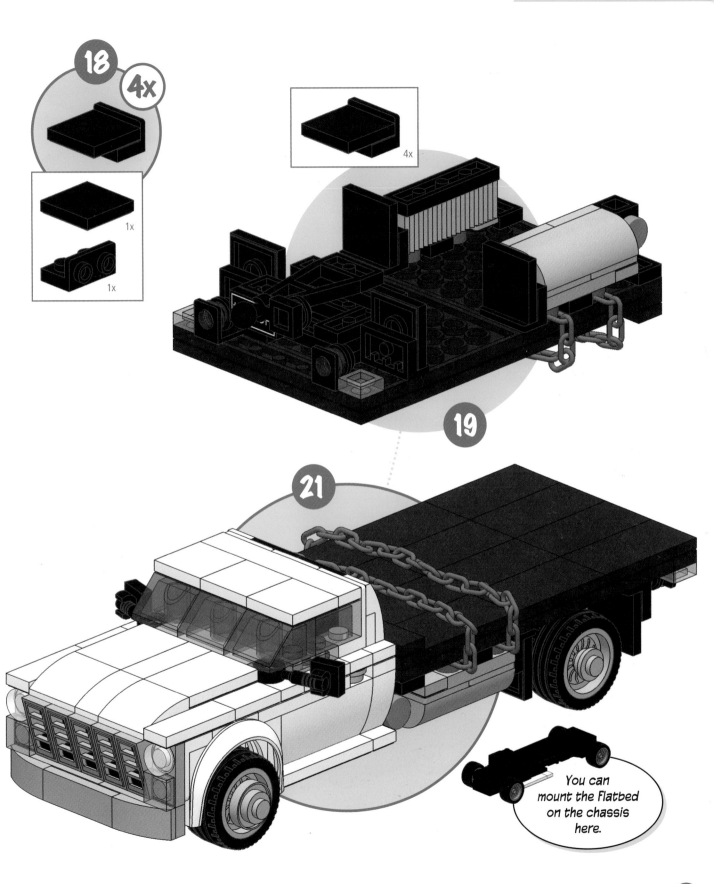

You can mount the Flatbed on the chassis here.

PARTS LIST

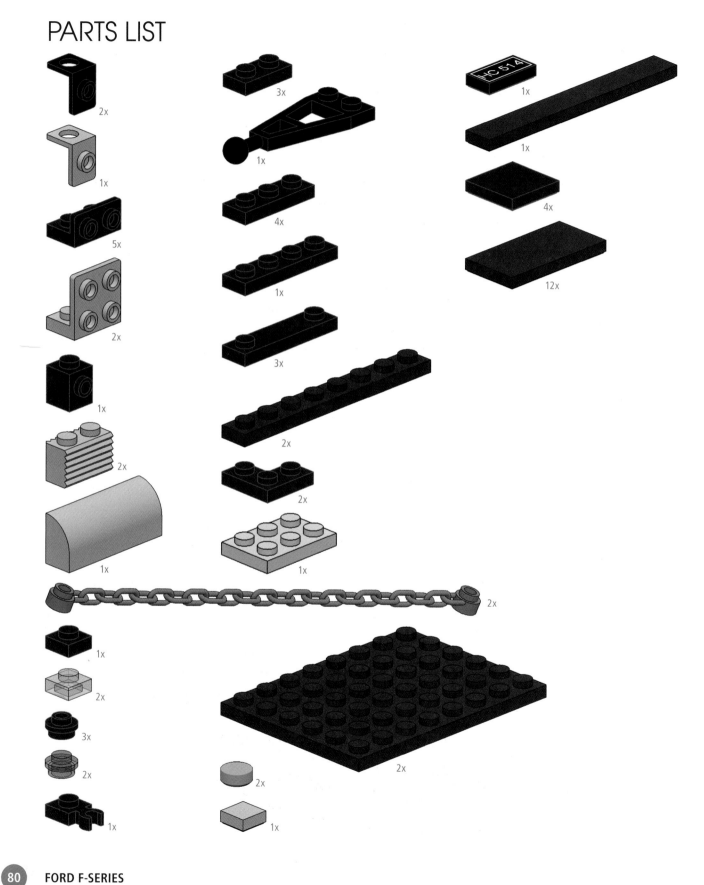

Amount	Color		Part number	Name	LEGO® Part number
2		Black	42446	Bracket 1 x 1 - 1 x 1	4169047, 4261427, 6020192
1		Light Bluish Gray	42446	Bracket 1 x 1 - 1 x 1	4211760
5		Black	99780	Bracket 1 x 2 - 1 x 2 Up	6020193
2		Light Bluish Gray	99207	Bracket 1 x 2 - 2 x 2 Up	4654580
1		Black	87087	Brick 1 x 1 with Stud on 1 Side	4558954
2		Light Bluish Gray	2877	Brick 1 x 2 with Grille	4211383
1		Light Bluish Gray	6191	Brick 1 x 4 x 1.333 with Curved Top	4249188, 6007033, 6195463
2		Dark Bluish Gray	30104	Minifig Chain 17L (Complete)	4211035, 4516456, 4516717
1		Black	3024	Plate 1 x 1	302426
2		Trans Orange	3024	Plate 1 x 1	4542673, 6252040
3		Black	4073	Plate 1 x 1 Round	614126
2		Trans Red	4073	Plate 1 x 1 Round	3005741, 6208450
1		Black	60897	Plate 1 x 1 with Clip Vertical (Open O-Clip)	4550017, 4617547
3		Black	3023	Plate 1 x 2	302326
1		Black	2508	Plate 1 x 2 with 3L Extension and Towball	250826, 4274405
4		Black	3623	Plate 1 x 3	362326
1		Black	3710	Plate 1 x 4	371026
3		Black	92593	Plate 1 x 4 with Two Studs	4599499
2		Reddish Brown	3460	Plate 1 x 8	4216945
2		Black	2420	Plate 2 x 2 Corner	242026
1		Light Bluish Gray	3021	Plate 2 x 3	4211396
2		Reddish Brown	3036	Plate 6 x 8	4223729
2		Flat Silver	98138	Tile 1 x 1 Round with Groove	4655241
1		Light Bluish Gray	3070b	Tile 1 x 1 with Groove	4211415
1		Black	3069bpa1	Tile 1 x 2 with White "HC514" Pattern	
1		Reddish Brown	4162	Tile 1 x 8	4211278, 4501848, 4585337
4		Black	3068b	Tile 2 x 2 with Groove	306826
12		Reddish Brown	87079	Tile 2 x 4 with Groove	4579690

On the following pages you will find some variations, ideas, details and tricks for your own creations.

We show you some variations and tricks for your own models here.

■ Some models—for example our Super Duty or the F-350—require a different wheelbase. If necessary, you can shorten it or make it wider quite easily.

■ The flatbed can also be built with print-ed wood tiles (*BL 2431pb415 / LEGO®
6151654*) or in other colors.

In our models we decided to use a differ-ent type of tire to the speed champion tires shown in the instructions. These are old tires from 1959–77, but are still often in circula-tion. You can find them under 132-hollow or 132old at BrickLink. When they first came out they were almost the only tires available. To-gether with the rim, they are also well suited for double tires.

With some small tags on the front, the Ford be-comes a Dodge. The round look of the radiator grille is achieved with a gray Rubber Belt Medium 3x3 (*BL x37 / LEGO® 71321 or 85544*).

At this point, it's a good idea to show you the light-ing system in more detail. It's possible to build it with a horizontal shaft (*BL 32828 / LEGO® 6196548*).

The typical gap between the cab and the loading area of a pickup can be achieved by installing a spacer. The centerpiece is the 1x3-thick Lift Arm (*BL 32523 / LEGO® 3252326 or 4142822*).

As it's possible to recognize the color through the grid tiles on the loading area, it's a good idea to color-match the spacer to the model.

In a 1976 Ford F-150, the front looks much older than in the 1978 model. As a typical feature of the bumper, we attached the Skates (*BL 93555 / LEGO® 4618133 or 6088641*) with a Technic Plate 1x5 (*BL 2711*).

With a little skill, you can even make a working tow truck. On the following two models, the Wrench (*BL 11402i / LEGO® 6030875*) was also used as a rear-view mirror. Here it is a tire holder for the vehicle being towed ...

... or a Four-Sided Sign with Snap on a dump truck (*BL 15210 / LEGO® 6063617*), which acts as a fender for the rear tires.

The tank is equipped with an obliquely mounted Fuel Cap (*BL 98138pb041 / LEGO® 6138964*).

Here are two examples of the latest minimized Speed Champion series Mudguards (fenders) in blue (*BL 35789 / LEGO® 6219820*) ...

... or in dark green (*BL 35789 / LEGO® 6217897*). That's pretty good for piecing together the woodland camouflage.

Here is a cabin from below and our idea for implementing the ambulance's power connection.

TILES

Now for the subtle details of the scene. You have already seen some of these backgrounds in the instructions. We didn't want to bother you with such details when you were reading the building instructions for the models, so we're only coming back to this now, since the use of various tiles is essential in this respect.

■ CAMERA / CHAIN BARRIER

It's pretty easy to put together a surveillance camera. An unprinted Microphone (*BL 90370 / LEGO® 6088550*) is perfect for this. This element also works wonderfully as a door handle or fence post.

ROAD SURFACE MARKINGS

If you wanted to create road surface markings in the old days, you had to build a wall and lay it flat. You can also create manhole covers this way (*BL 4150ps4 / LEGO® 4221881*).

Nowadays you can get triangular tiles (*BL 35787 / LEGO® 6217875 white, 6217876 gray*), which you can use to build arrows evenly without 'snotting' (*SNOT = Stud Not On Top*). Unfortunately, this solution isn't as yet available for manhole covers, as there is no round tile to use for the cover. You can see how we used this technique on the next double-page spread, in our underground parking lot, although Kavinsky and his recently parked Ferrari might distract you.

Try and think about your own patterns and ornaments!

▍FLOOR PATTERN

You can play with creating all sorts of different shapes with various new tiles—for example, with this angular beveled tile (*BL 27263 / LEGO® dbg 6177079, lbg 6177078*).

MODEL KIT

Many observers have been amazed by this display because it looks like a model kit at first.

By the way, the tiles with the imprinted rule come from set 5005107 (*Buildable Ruler*)—hopefully that answers a frequently asked question.

A photo for the construction of the brushes can be found on page 120.

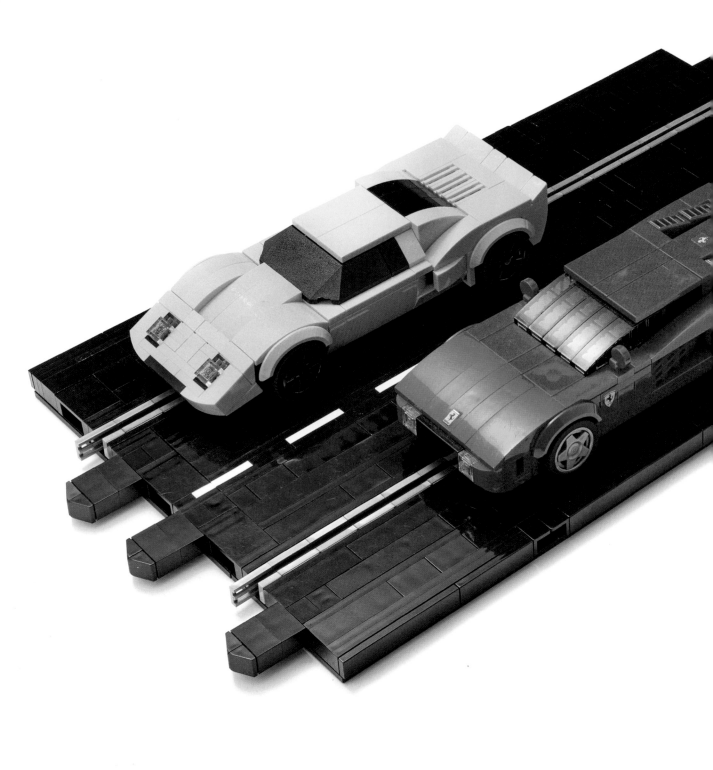

FORD GT 40

A racing legend! We really wanted to use the square windshield for a model. And then we also wanted to create a streamlined race car. The building instructions are suitable for a mono-chrome version, but you can also use them for a version with a strip down the middle.

1

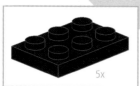
5x

2x   1x

2

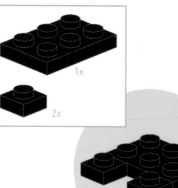
1x

2x

3

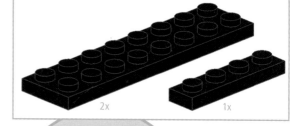

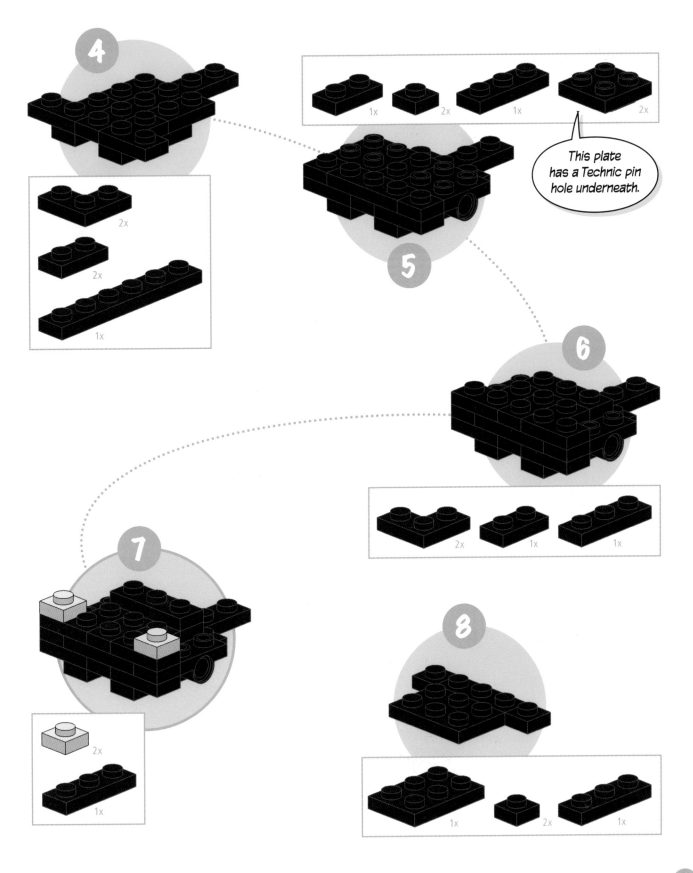

This plate has a Technic pin hole underneath.

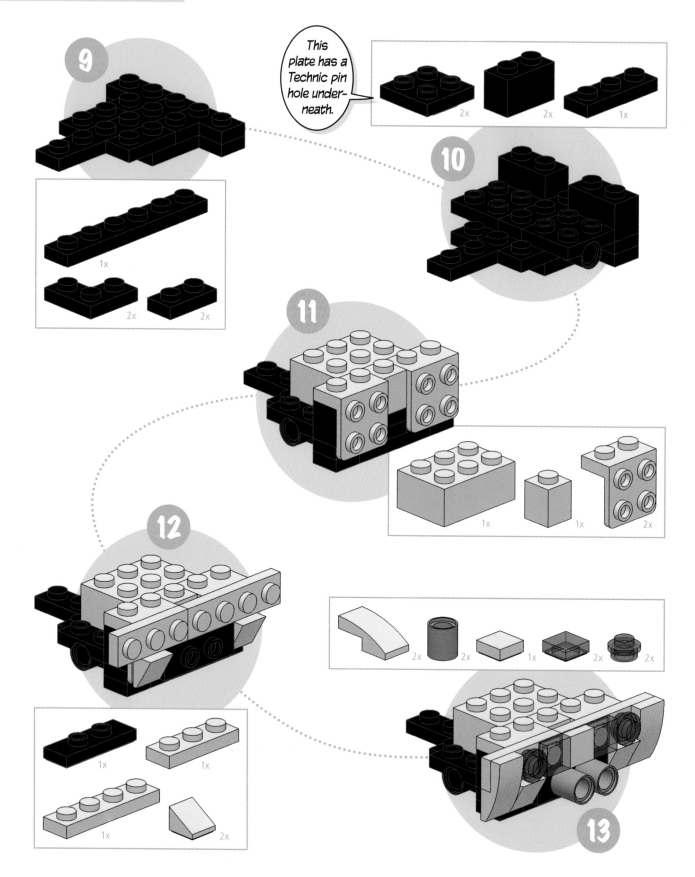

This plate has a Technic pin hole underneath.

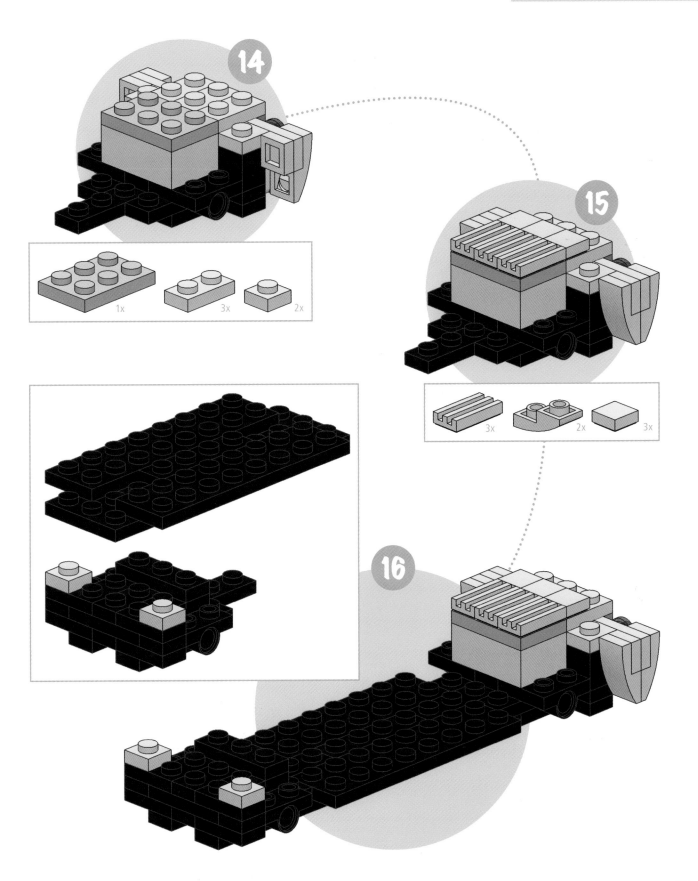

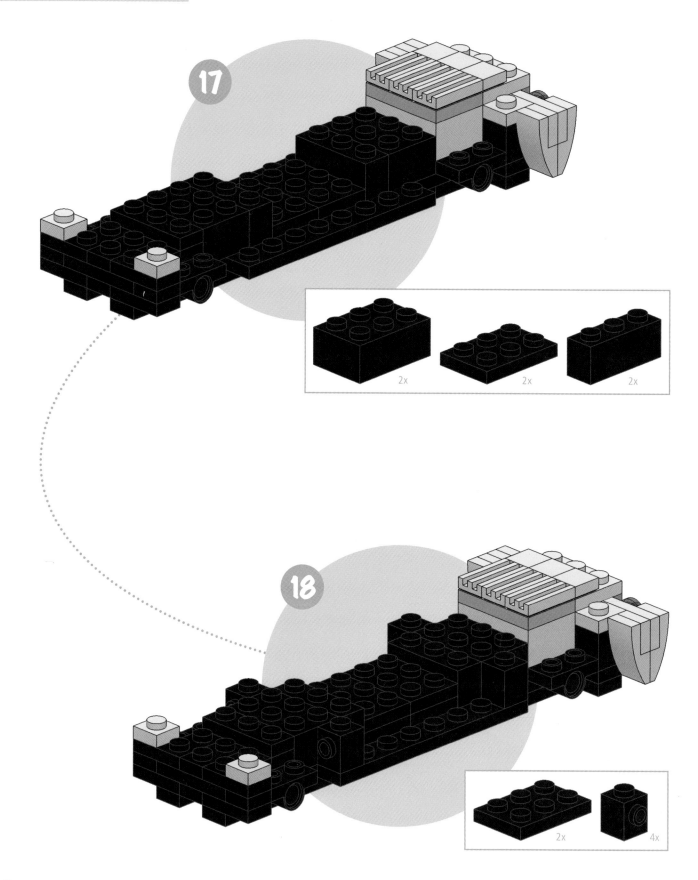

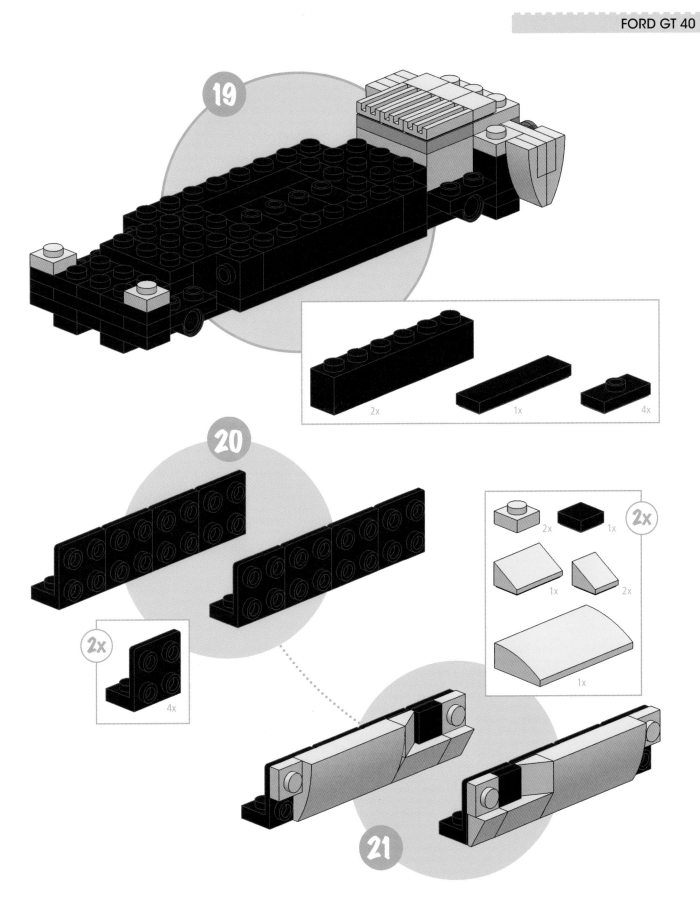

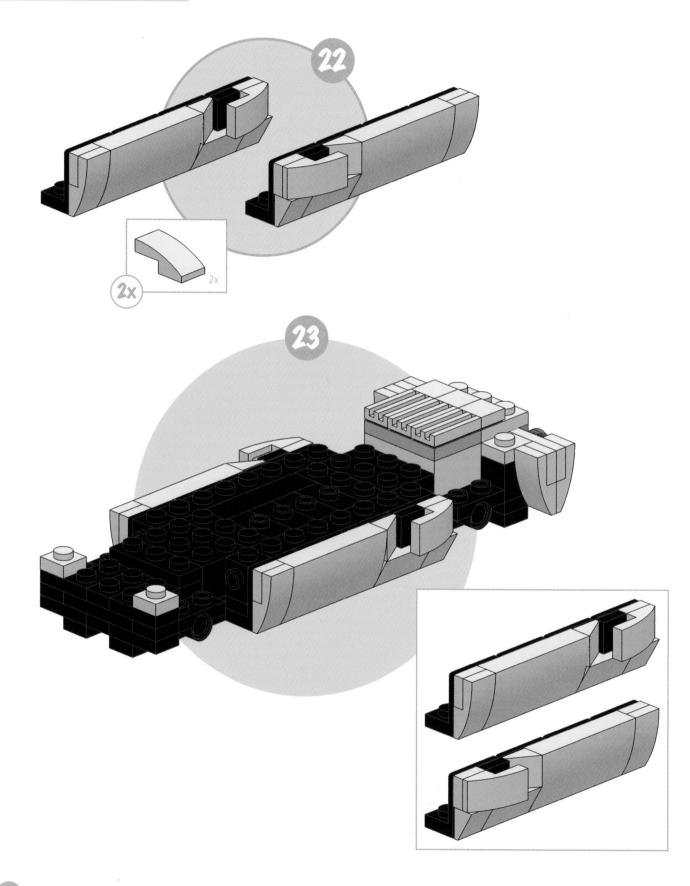

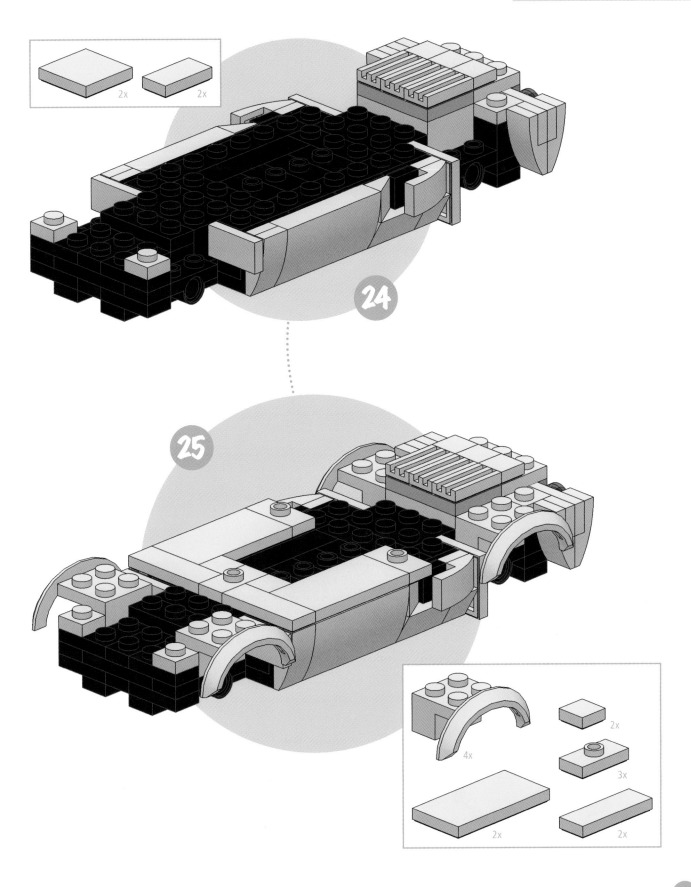

24

25

2x
2x

4x

2x

3x

2x
2x

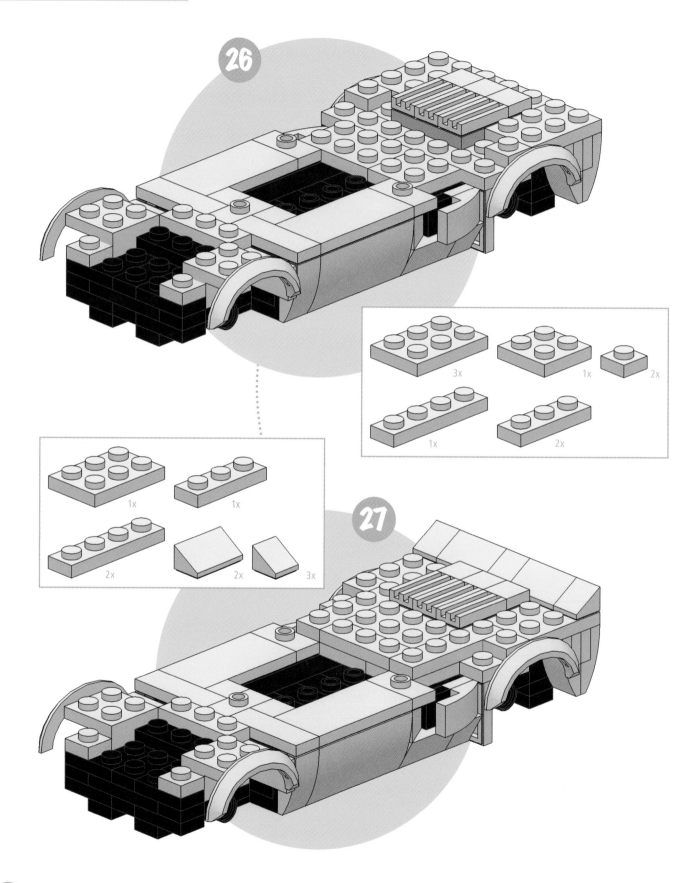

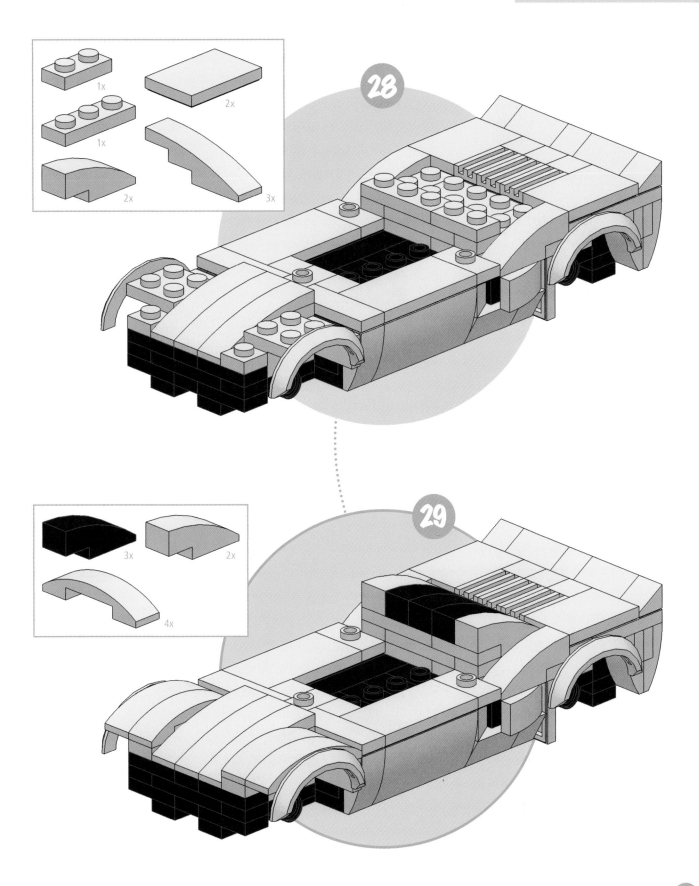

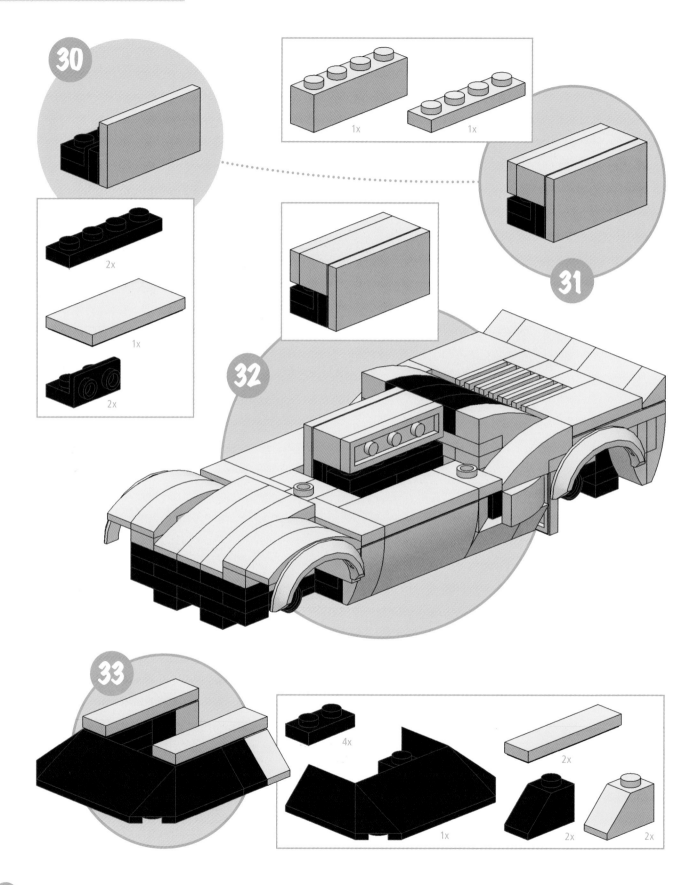

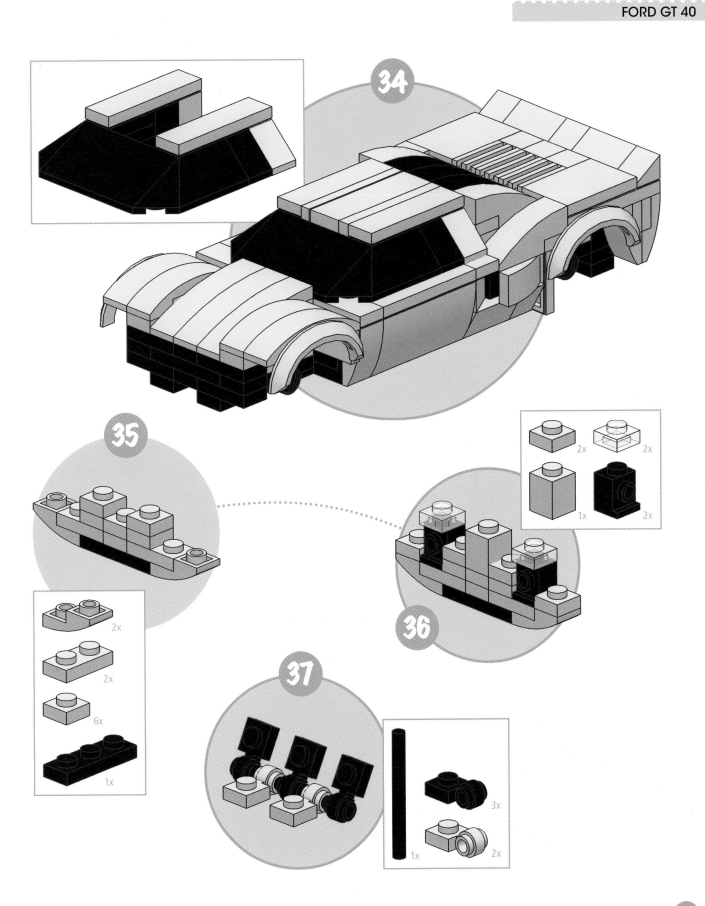

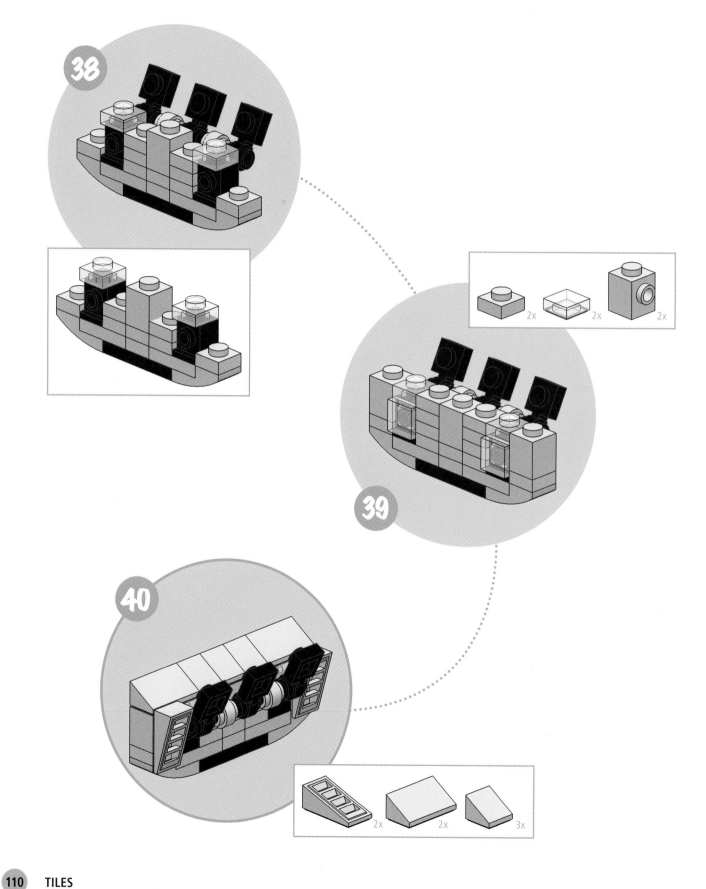

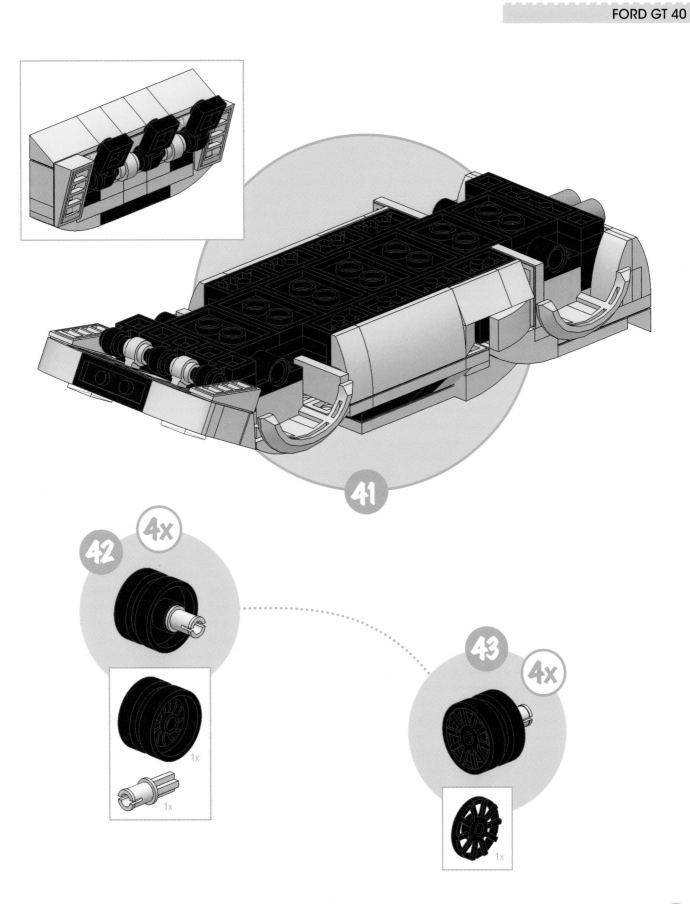

41

42 4x

43 4x

1x

1x

1x

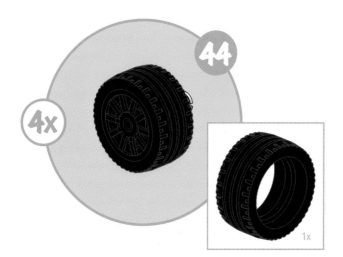

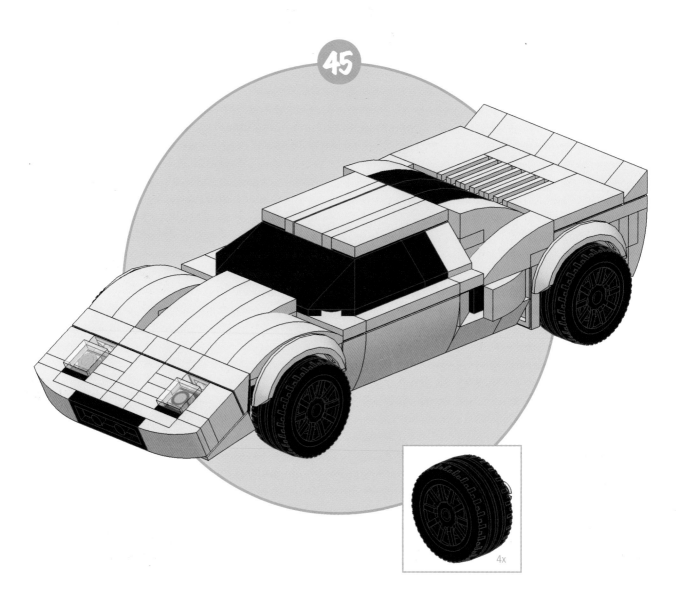

PARTS LIST

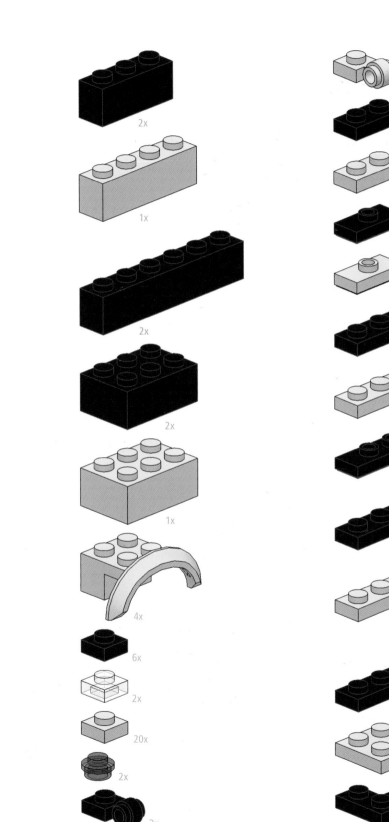

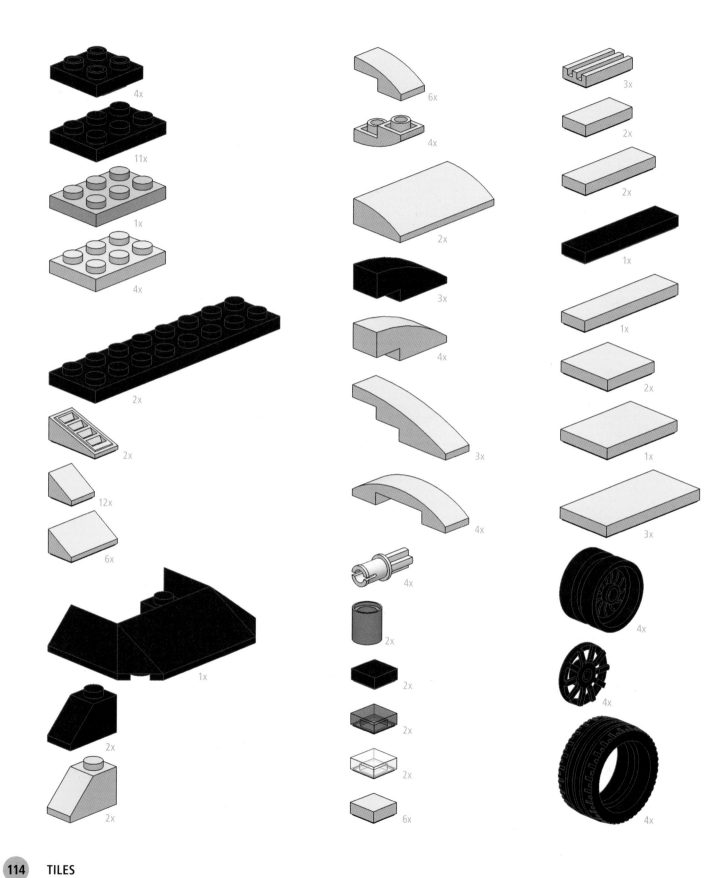

Amount	Color		Part number	Name	LEGO® Part number
1		Black	30374	Bar 4L Lightsaber Blade	3037426, 4140303, 6116604
2		Black	99780	Bracket 1 x 2 - 1 x 2 Up	6020193
2		Yellow	44728	Bracket 1 x 2 - 2 x 2	4199298, 4277925, 4615642, 6117938
8		Black	99207	Bracket 1 x 2 - 2 x 2 Up	6000650
2		Yellow	3005	Brick 1 x 1	300524
2		Black	4070	Brick 1 x 1 with Headlight	407026
4		Black	87087	Brick 1 x 1 with Stud on 1 Side	4558954
2		Yellow	87087	Brick 1 x 1 with Stud on 1 Side	4624985
2		Black	3004	Brick 1 x 2	300426
2		Black	3622	Brick 1 x 3	362226
1		Yellow	3010	Brick 1 x 4	301024
2		Black	3009	Brick 1 x 6	300926
2		Black	3002	Brick 2 x 3	300226
1		Yellow	3002	Brick 2 x 3	300224
4		Yellow	98282	Car Mudguard 4 x 2.5 x 1	6096999
6		Black	3024	Plate 1 x 1	302426
2		Trans Clear	3024	Plate 1 x 1	3000840, 6252041
20		Yellow	3024	Plate 1 x 1	302424
2		Trans Red	4073	Plate 1 x 1 Round	3005741, 6208450
3		Black	4081b	Plate 1 x 1 with Clip Light Type 2	408126, 4632571
2		Yellow	4081b	Plate 1 x 1 with Clip Light Type 2	408124, 4632569
10		Black	3023	Plate 1 x 2	302326
6		Yellow	3023	Plate 1 x 2	302324
4		Black	3794b	Plate 1 x 2 with Groove with 1 Centre Stud	379426
3		Yellow	3794b	Plate 1 x 2 with Groove with 1 Centre Stud	379424
6		Black	3623	Plate 1 x 3	362326
5		Yellow	3623	Plate 1 x 3	362324
1		Black	34103	Plate 1 x 3 with 2 Studs Offset	6199908
3		Black	3710	Plate 1 x 4	371026
5		Yellow	3710	Plate 1 x 4	371024
2		Black	3666	Plate 1 x 6	366626
1		Yellow	3022	Plate 2 x 2	302224, 4613978
6		Black	2420	Plate 2 x 2 Corner	242026
4		Black	10247	Plate 2 x 2 with Hole and Complete Underside Rib	6061032
11		Black	3021	Plate 2 x 3	302126
1		Light Bluish Gray	3021	Plate 2 x 3	4211396
4		Yellow	3021	Plate 2 x 3	302124

Amount	Color	Part number	Name	LEGO® Part number
2	Black	3034	Plate 2 x 8	303426
2	Yellow	61409	Slope Brick 18 2 x 1 x 0.667 Grille	4521167, 4540384
12	Yellow	54200	Slope Brick 31 1 x 1 x 0.667	4283095, 4504381
6	Yellow	85984	Slope Brick 31 1 x 2 x 0.667	4550348
1	Black	13269	Slope Brick 33/45 6 x 4 with 2 x 2 Cutout	6031790
2	Black	3040	Slope Brick 45 2 x 1	304026, 4121966
2	Yellow	3040	Slope Brick 45 2 x 1	304024, 4121965
6	Yellow	11477	Slope Brick Curved 2 x 1	6029947
4	Yellow	24201	Slope Brick Curved 2 x 1 Inverted	6167223
2	Yellow	88930	Slope Brick Curved 2 x 4 with Underside Studs	4597902
3	Black	50950	Slope Brick Curved 3 x 1	4251161
4	Yellow	50950	Slope Brick Curved 3 x 1	4247771
3	Yellow	61678	Slope Brick Curved 4 x 1	4522035, 6024715
4	Yellow	93273	Slope Brick Curved 4 x 1 Double	4613151
4	Tan	3749	Technic Axle Pin	4186017, 4666579, 65625
2	Flat Silver	18654	Technic Beam 1	6161155
2	Black	3070b	Tile 1 x 1 with Groove	307026
2	Trans Black	3070b	Tile 1 x 1 with Groove	4529684, 6038458
2	Trans Clear	3070b	Tile 1 x 1 with Groove	4162145, 6047501
6	Yellow	3070b	Tile 1 x 1 with Groove	307024
3	Yellow	2412b	Tile 1 x 2 Grille with Groove	241224
2	Yellow	3069b	Tile 1 x 2 with Groove	306924
2	Yellow	63864	Tile 1 x 3 with Groove	4558172
1	Black	2431	Tile 1 x 4 with Groove	243126
2	Yellow	2431	Tile 1 x 4 with Groove	243124
2	Yellow	3068b	Tile 2 x 2 with Groove	306824
2	Yellow	26603	Tile 2 x 3	
3	Yellow	87079	Tile 2 x 4	
4	Black	18976	Wheel 18mm D. x 12mm with Axle Hole and Stud with Black Tire 24 x 12 low	18976, 18977
4	Black	18976b	Wheel Cover 10 Spoke - for Wheel	18976
4	Black	18977	Tire 24 x 12 low	

Here you can see how even a gray disk can also work really well. It's also a good idea to decorate the car with stickers from older sets.

SLOT RACETRACK

Anyone who has ever wondered how to build the elements for a slot (*page 96/97*) racetrack need only take a careful look at these pictures. Of course, we'll also give you a few numbers here you can use to order them, for example the big black 8x16 tile (*BL 90498 / LEGO® 4603646*).

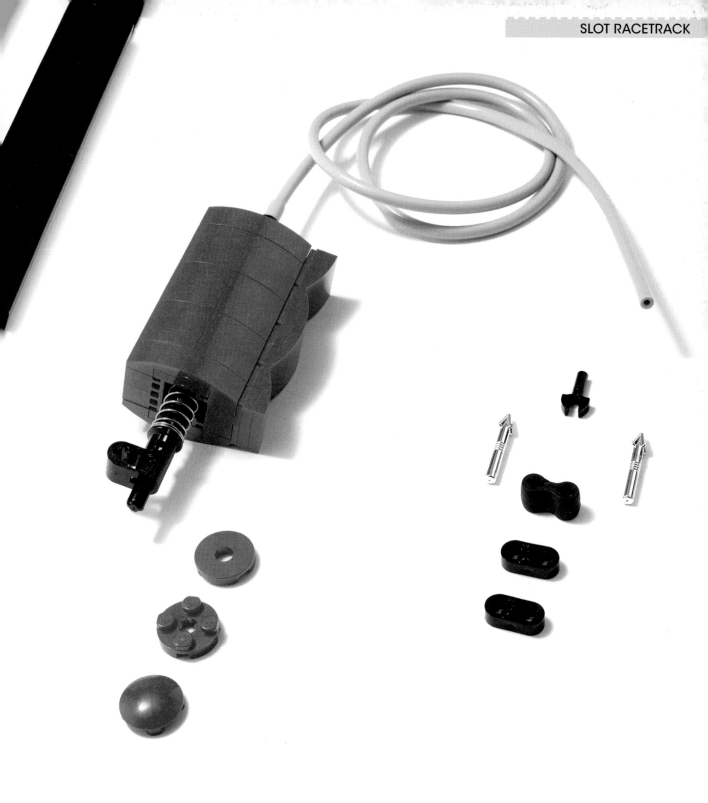

The pneumatic hose used as cable is available in different lengths. Here we used the longest available one at 71.2 cm / 38 in (*BL 5102c89*). Not that we want you to think we've been misusing parts! Naturally, you can get shorter hoses and different colors.

▊BRUSH

Going back to our model kit (*page 95*), the brush and scalpel shown here can be assembled in a similar way, so we're showing only one of them in exploded view.

ROUND 2x2 TILES

Round 2x2 tiles can be joined in two directions by using the trick of simply clamping two bars with clips (*BL 48729b / LEGO® 4289538*) between two round tiles, for example for a public clock at the station.

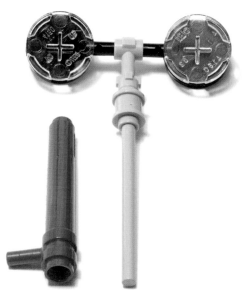

The same technique lets you build the emergency light for one of our emergency vehicles. Together with the Cylinder 1x5½ with Handle (*BL 87617 / LEGO® 4565432 or 6195914*), this is also retractable.

There are several round stickers in the LEGO® assortment that you can use to design a barrier. Here are two suggestions: "Stop" from set 5970 (*BL 5970stk01*) and "No entry" (*BL 8196stk02*).

"Starting point" for this simu-
lated model cast-iron frame follows the same pattern.

The trick also works with round
plates and anything that has a
clip—like this Finger Leaf (*BL 10884
/ LEGO® 6020157*). Here we turned
over a bush and connected it to two
palm leaves and a round 2x2 plate to
give our palm a realistic substructure
of dead leaves.

Here you can see the light pole again, as we mounted it on our Fire & Rescue emergency vehicle. In this shot from the back of the vehicle you also have a good view of the taillights. We will show you its structure in detail in the next exploded view.

CURVED TILES

Round tiles and larger curved tiles: As you can see on the preceding double-page spread, you can use these to create amazingly clear tire tracks in the snow.

You can even use them to create a round bench beautifully. For the feet, we used the new 1x2 Rounded Plate (*BL 35480 / LEGO® 6210270*). The curves give a really good overall look.

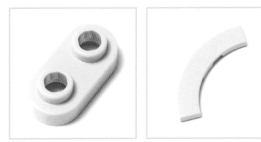

And since this 1x2 board (BL 35480 / LEGO® 6210270) has holes in the studs, a 1x2 board can be placed in the bottom stud in the middle of the lamp. It's a perfect solution for the series designation on the door of a steam locomotive's smokebox.

The edge of a cup can be put together in the scale
shown here by using the 1x1 brick with two studs
at 90 degrees (*BL 26604 / LEGO® 6175968*).

HEADLAMPS

In the movie The Italian Job (*2003*) a security van falls into a subway shaft, where its contents are then loaded into waiting Minis. We've given our Minis glowing headlamps so they see where they are going. The fenders have been designed so that a Glow in the Dark white Lightsaber bar (*BL 30374 / LEGO® 6009094*) can be inserted into four modified plates (*BL 11458 / LEGO® 6099736 red*).

The new half bracket (*BL 36840 / LEGO® 6225494*) makes it easy to build a step into the radiator, where you can also use a black grille. The 2x2 tiles with two studs are handy for the side sills.

PALLET

Building a small pallet is not difficult at all. The printed 1x6 tile (*BL 6636px1*) is unfortunately relatively rare, but an unprinted one will also work.

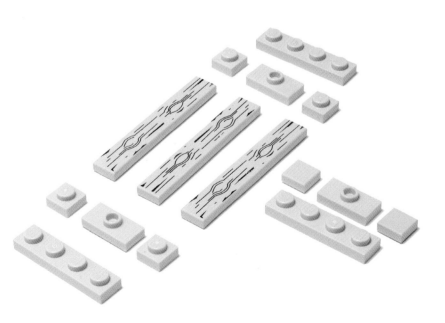

EMERGENCY EXIT

Fine details such as emergency exit lighting or railings can also be built. We'll show you how in these two exploded-view photos.

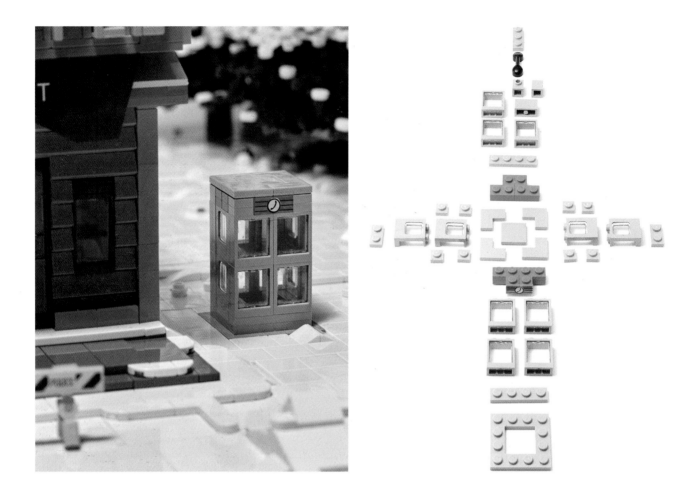

▎TELEPHONE BOOTH

An old telephone booth from the 1980s can be found next to the waffle hut of our scene from the US TV series Fargo (*2014–*). The 4x4 Frame Plate (*BL 64799 / LEGO® 4612621*) provides its stability. We never thought we would consider this element important.

The roof is made of four tile-covered 2x2 angle tiles (*BL 14719 / LEGO® 6065824*).

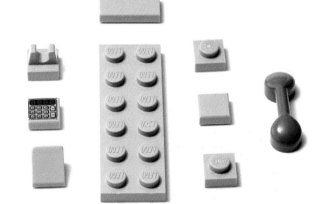

The "Aston Martin DB5" (*10262*) set contains a brand-new element—an Outside Half Bow (*BL 37352 / LEGO® 6227184*)—that made it possible to build this telephone column at very short notice before the photo shoot for this book.

▌BARRIER

You may have already seen it in the picture, but here it is again: a police barrier.

It's simple but effective. The stand should not be too big. Bar Holders with Clip (*BL 11090 / LEGO® 6015892*) are very good as mainstays. The sticker comes from set 60007 (*BL 60007stk01*).

Nee-naw ...

LIGHTING SYSTEM

On the previous pages, we have already shown you one way to build a lighting system for an ambulance or emergency vehicle. Now we would like to show you another, more fine-grained attachment that we developed for our model of a Minnesota State Patrol police car.

LANTERNS

LEGO® bricks can be used to build a wide variety of lanterns and lamps. For our Fargo lantern, a Modified 1x1 Rounded with Handle (*BL 26047 / LEGO® 6157554*) and a Technic Pin (*BL 15100 / LEGO® 6073231*) are the most important components.

We have completely different street lighting on the Walk of Fame. Here, a small cone (*BL 85975 / LEGO® 4619597 or 6203937*) connects the base to the mast.

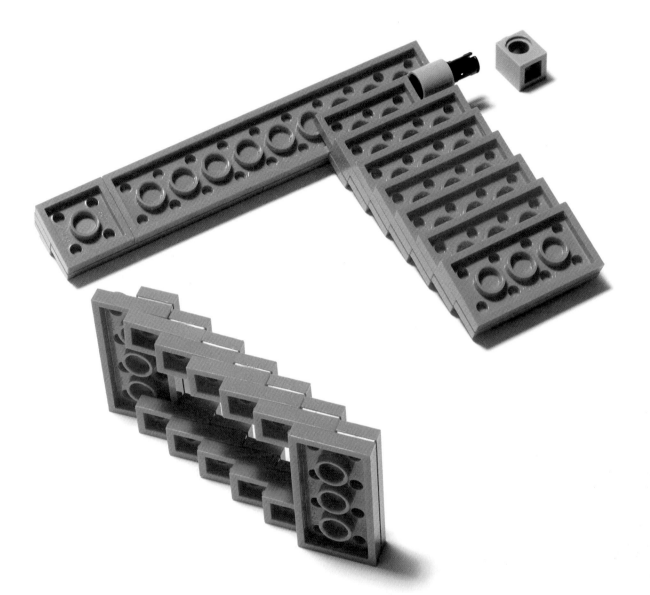

WOODEN LAGGING

The wooden lagging of our Waffle Hut is in US Western style. At first glance, the design looks more complicated than it actually is.

The modified plate shown earlier (*BL 18677 / LEGO®6168633*) is also available in inverse, meaning that the studs point in the other direction. You only have to make a quick calculation or try out the spacing of the elements that fit your model.

PLANTS

This drive-in was inspired by the movie classic American Graffiti. We also want to use it to show you some techniques and tricks including how to include lettering and other such details.
First, do look at our palm tree! We want to show you how you can build the most diverse plants and planters.

▌PALM TREE

You've already seen the top of our palm on page 122. Another nice detail is the rattles (*BL 90301* / *LEGO® 4610065*) that we've used as coconuts here.

You can achieve a bent palm trunk by fitting a rigid 3-mm trouser piece (*BL 75c17*) into the trunk. This way, you can move the cones while the trunk remains stable because it is "secured" inside.

We assembled the planter with a 3x3 Plate (*BL 11212 / LEGO® 6015347*), 2x3 Flat Tiles (*BL 23603 / LEGO® 6156667*), and a modified Brick 1x2 with Studs (*BL 11211 / LEGO® 6058177*).

■ POTTED PLANT

For this slightly smaller version of a plant pot, we used a golden ring (*BL 11010 / LEGO® 6009771*). It has quite a lot of visual impact and also works with a snot connection (*SNOT = Studs Not On Top*) —it's made possible by connecting two hollow studs. When you use studs with lettering, the distance between the studs increases slightly and makes the whole structure a bit wobbly.

WEEPING WILLOW

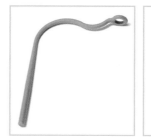
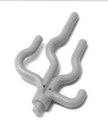

We found this weeping willow rather touching. However, you have to own quite a lot of Whips (*BL 2488 / LEGO® 248828 or 6055462*) and Sea Grass (*BL 30093 / LEGO® 4163425 or 4568215*) to make it.

CACTUS

Here's one plant that looks really good with studs — the cactus.

Naturally, you can stylize it too, as we did here in our bumper cars scene. We used cheese corners for the arms (*Quarter Circle Tile 1x1: BL 25269 / LEGO® 6150607*) and 1x1 semicircle tiles.

MILNER'S COUPE

Did you notice the so-called "Milner Coupe" in the scene at Mel's Drive-In? It's a 1932 Ford converted into a hot rod and driven by John Milner in American Graffiti (1973).
The fenders can be installed diagonally with two old finger joints (*BL 2452 / LEGO® 4276*). You can see this quite well on the photo of the car taken from below.

Small details make the difference.

▇ WINDSHIELDS

We equipped the two vintage cars in the same scene with really old wind-shields (*BL x453*) that are slightly curved.

SMALL OIL-POWERED SHUNTING LOCOMOTIVE 1 (KÖ I)

The two most common questions at exhibitions so far have been what "Kö I" stands for in German and whether we have building instructions for the model. Here are the instructions and our answer: "Kö I" stands for "Kleinlokomotive, ölbefeuert, der Leistungsgruppe 1" (*small, oil-fired locomotive in performance group 1*) (*up to 40hp*). In Germany, it was first put into service for light shunting tasks for the former German Reichsbahn (*DR*) in 1930.

If you prefer using the 9-volt electric engine instead of building a sliding locomotive, you can skip the steps 31–36 of the building instructions for the undercarriage and use this engine instead (*BL 590 / Lego® 70358*):

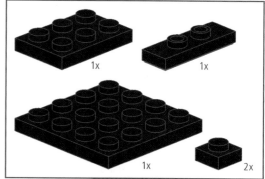

1

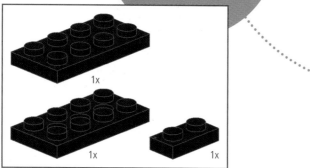

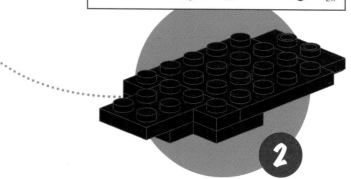

2

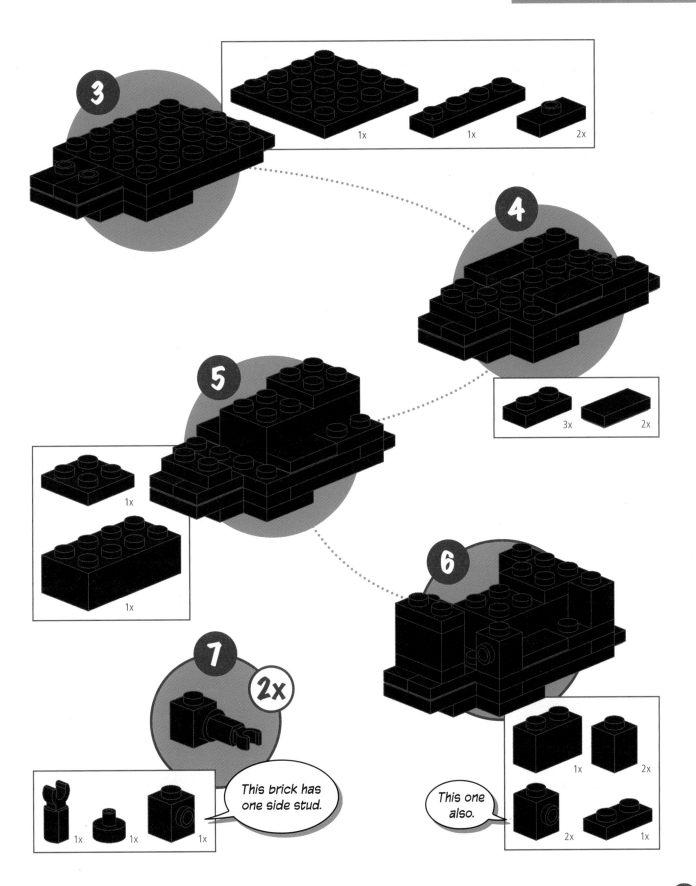

This brick has one side stud.

This one also.

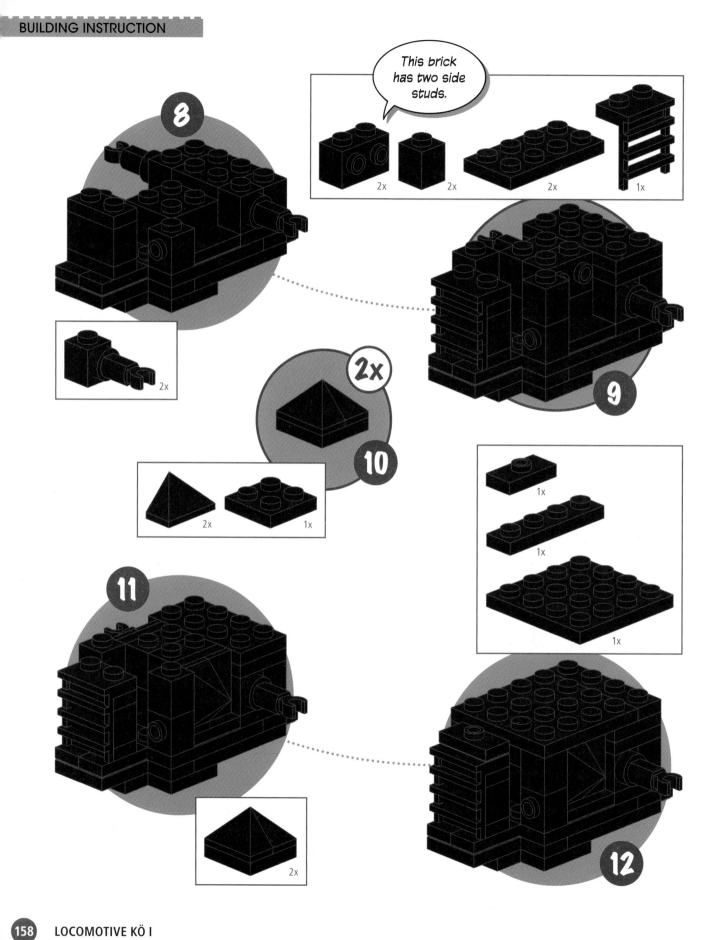

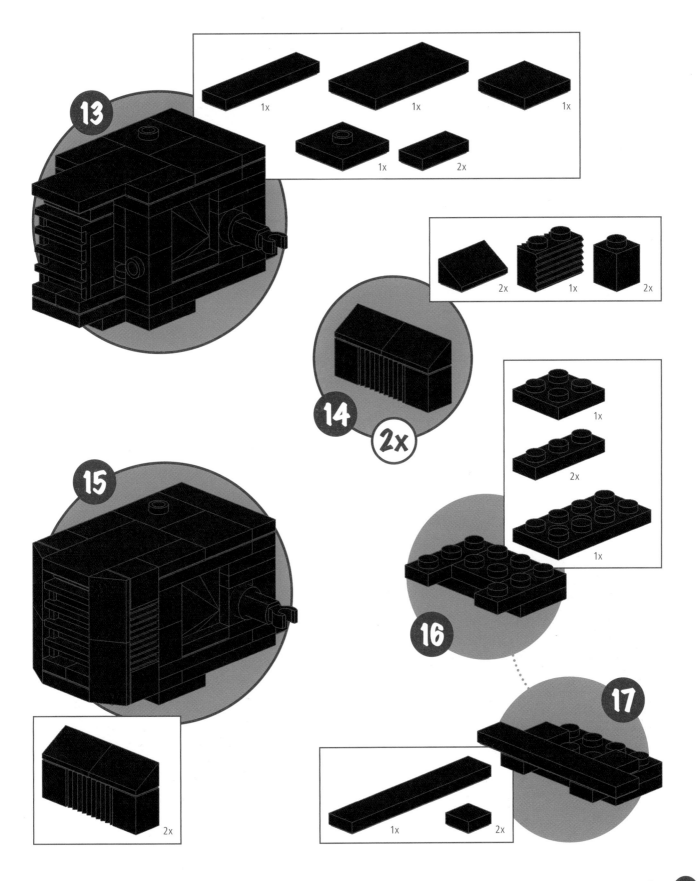

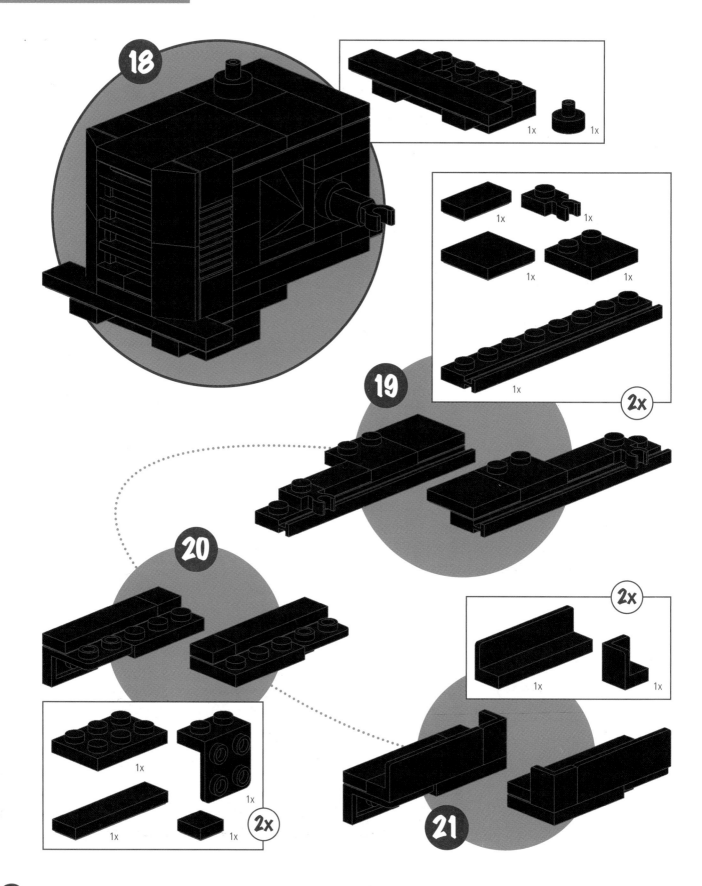

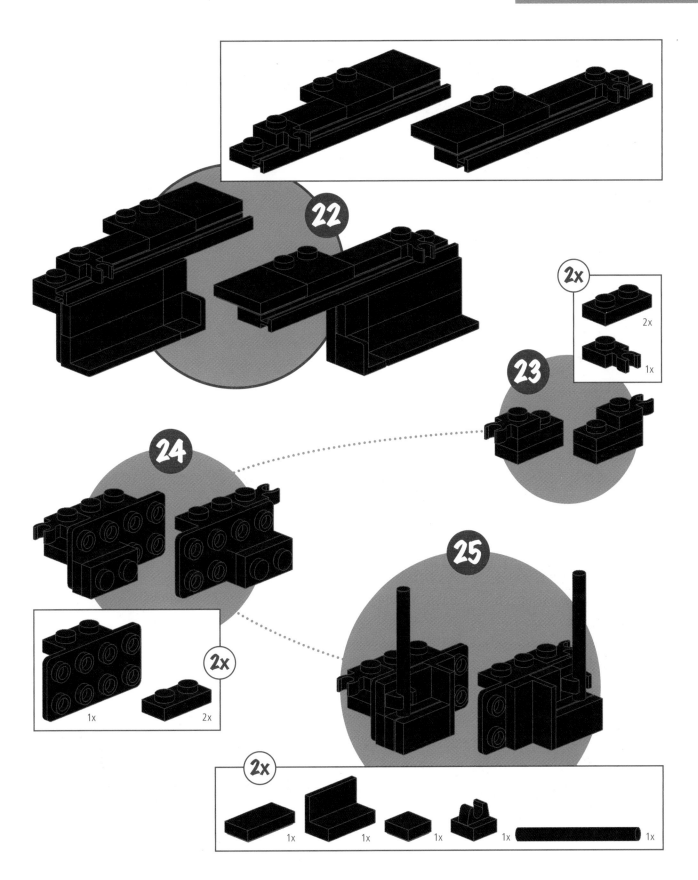

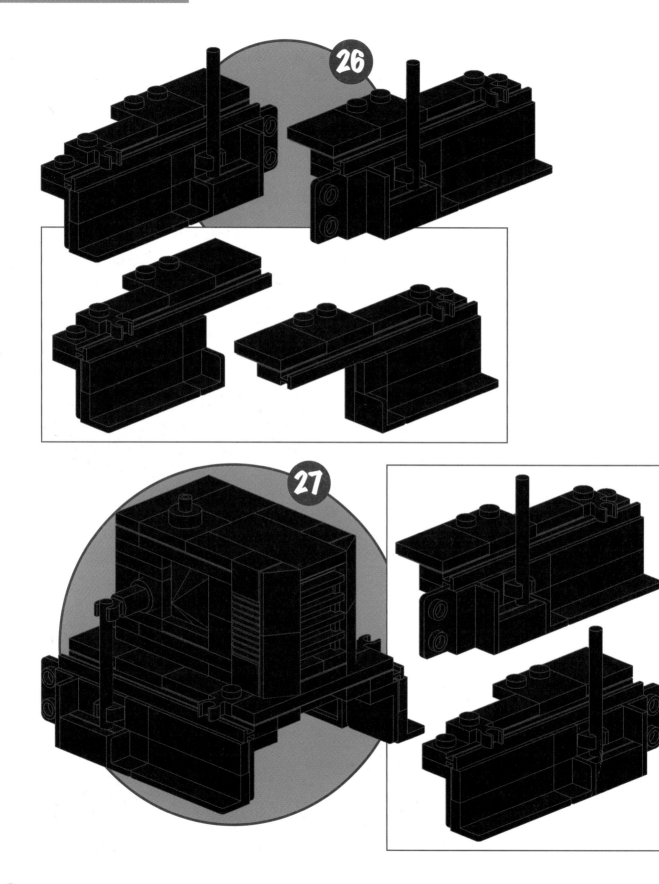

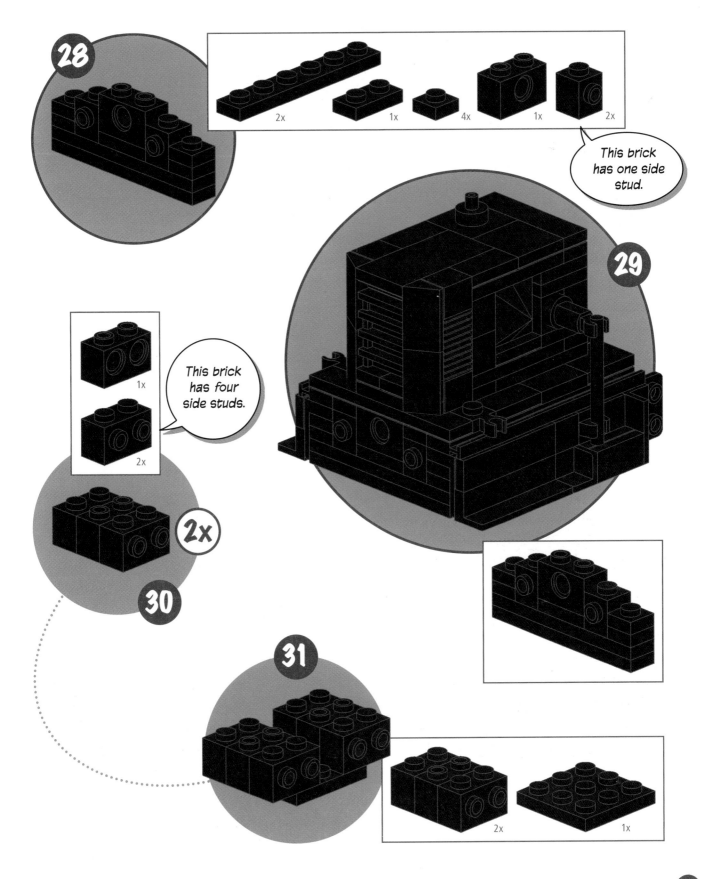

This brick has one side stud.

This brick has four side studs.

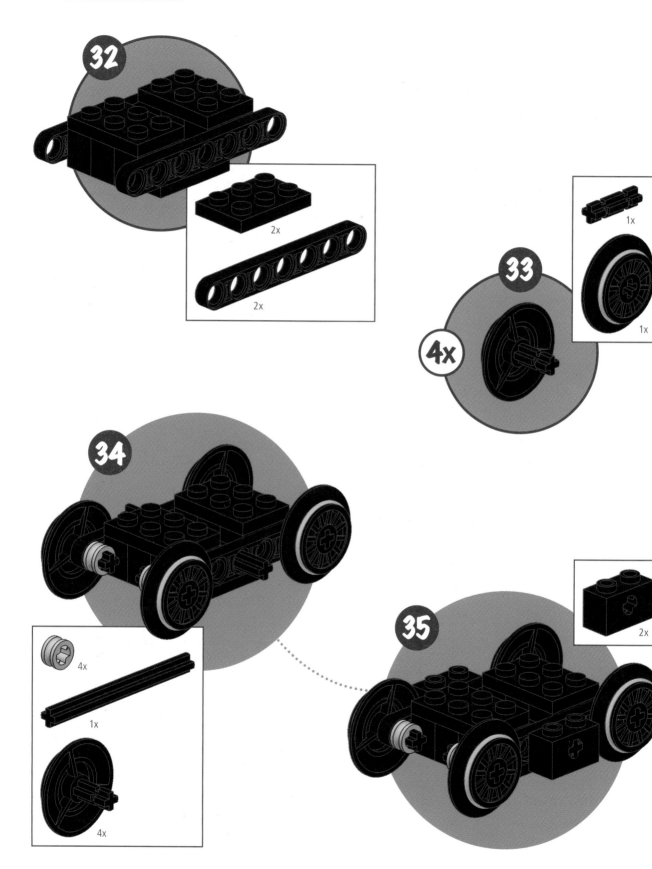

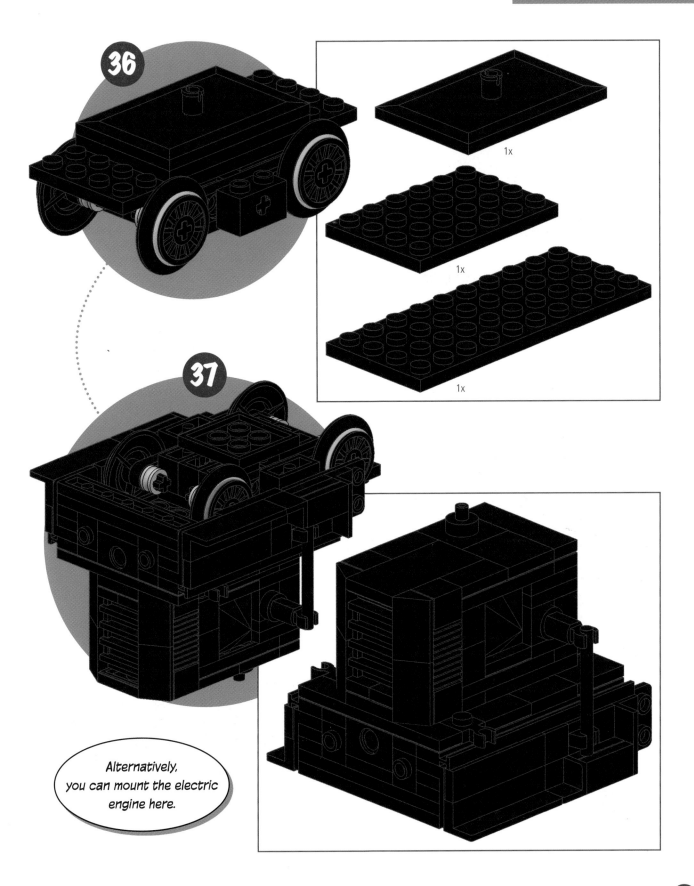

36

1x

1x

1x

37

Alternatively, you can mount the electric engine here.

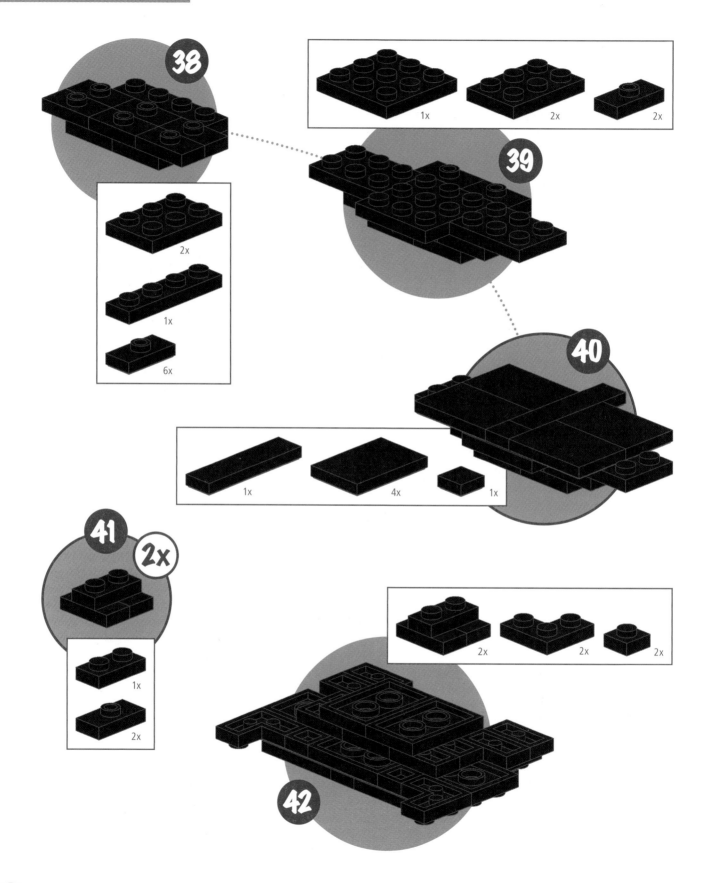

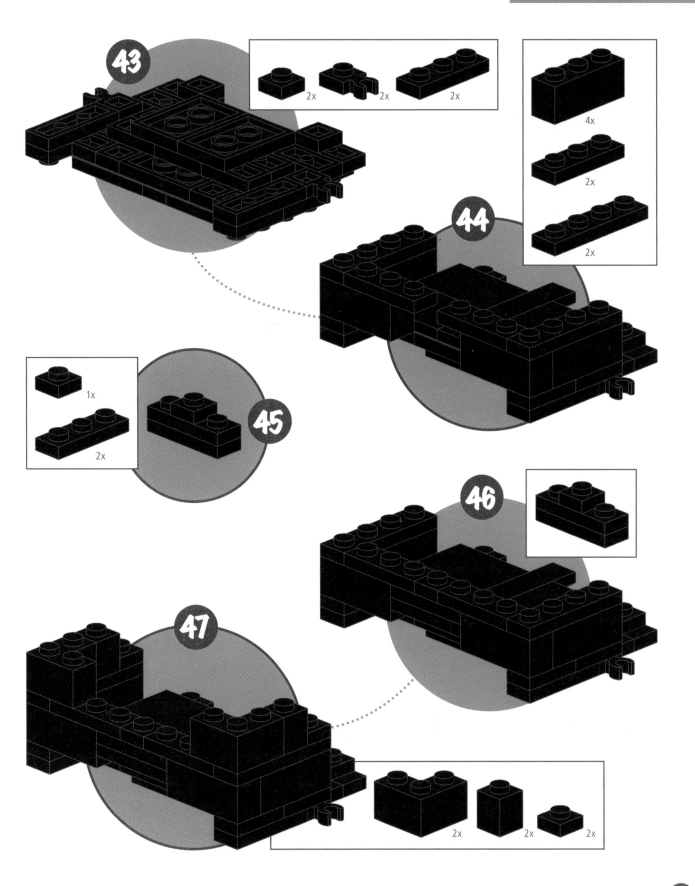

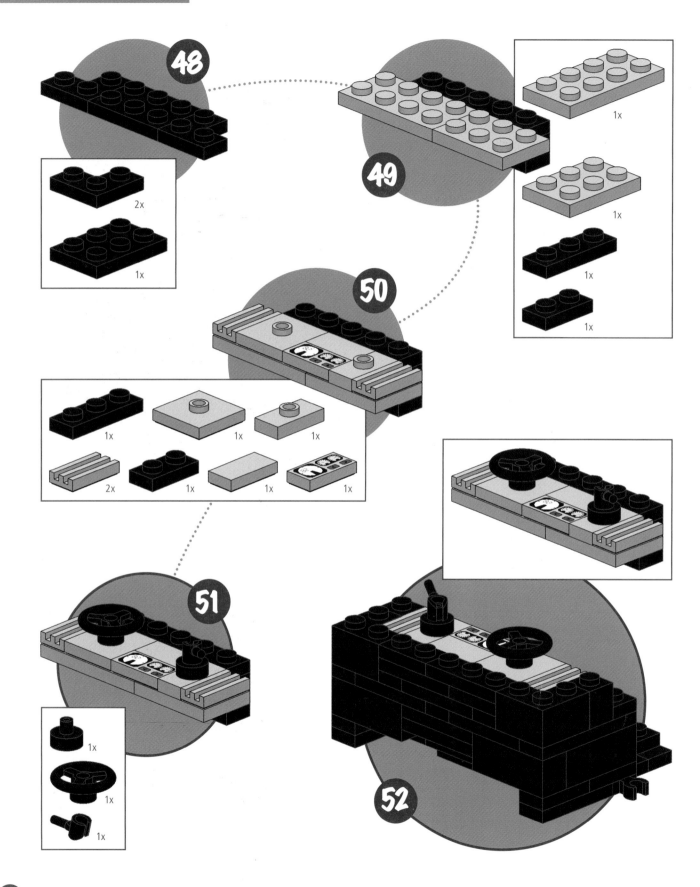

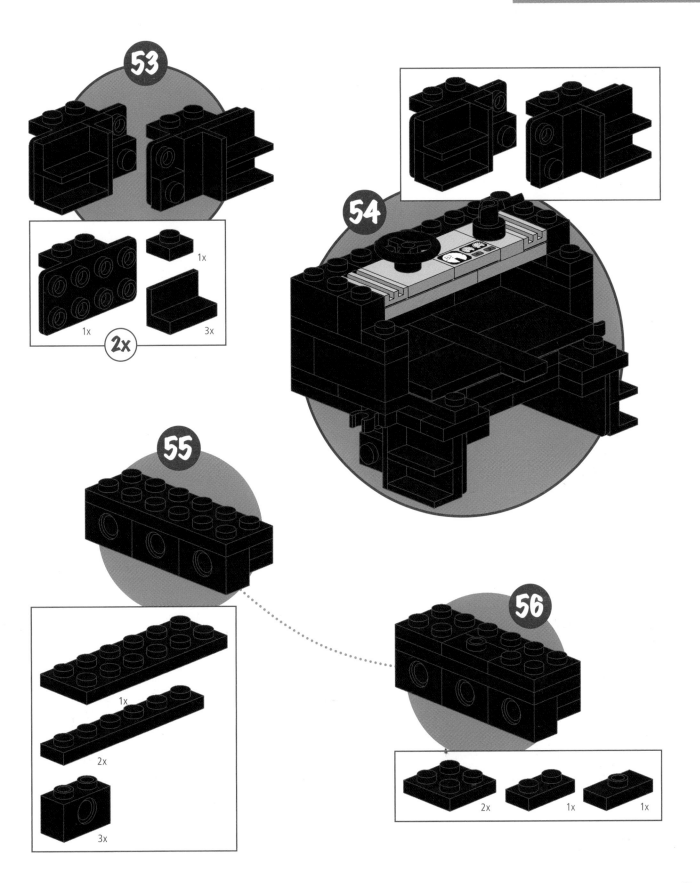

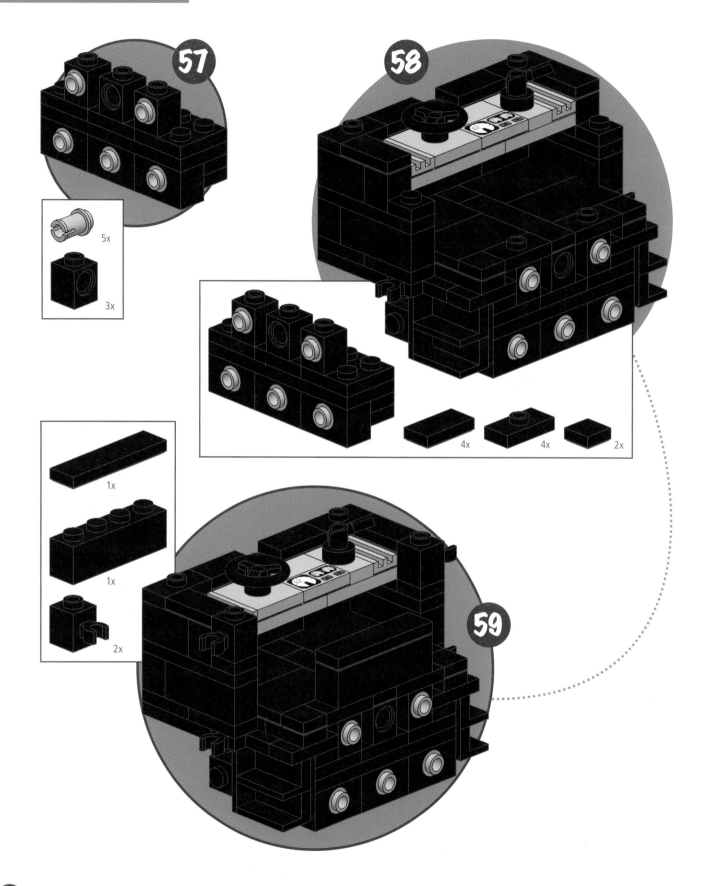

57

5x

3x

58

4x

4x

2x

1x

1x

2x

59

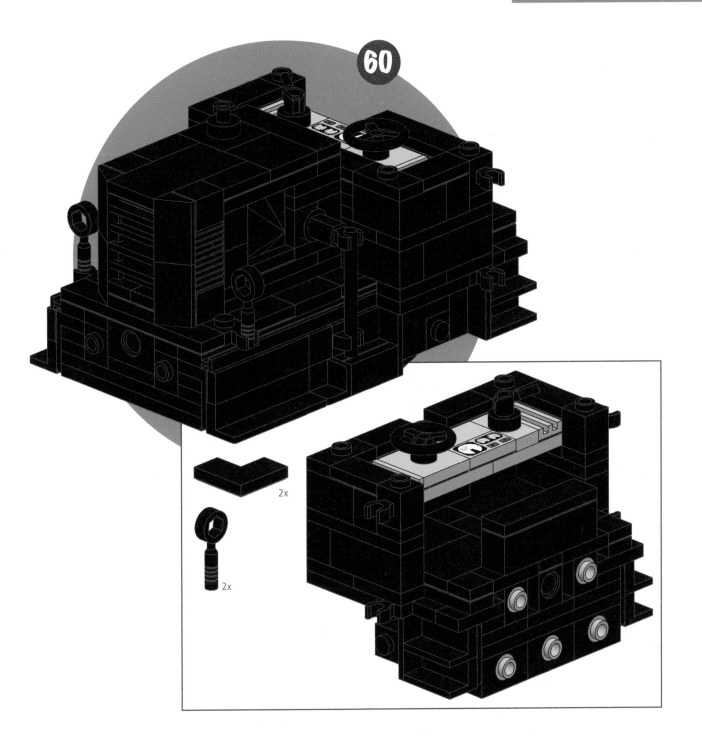

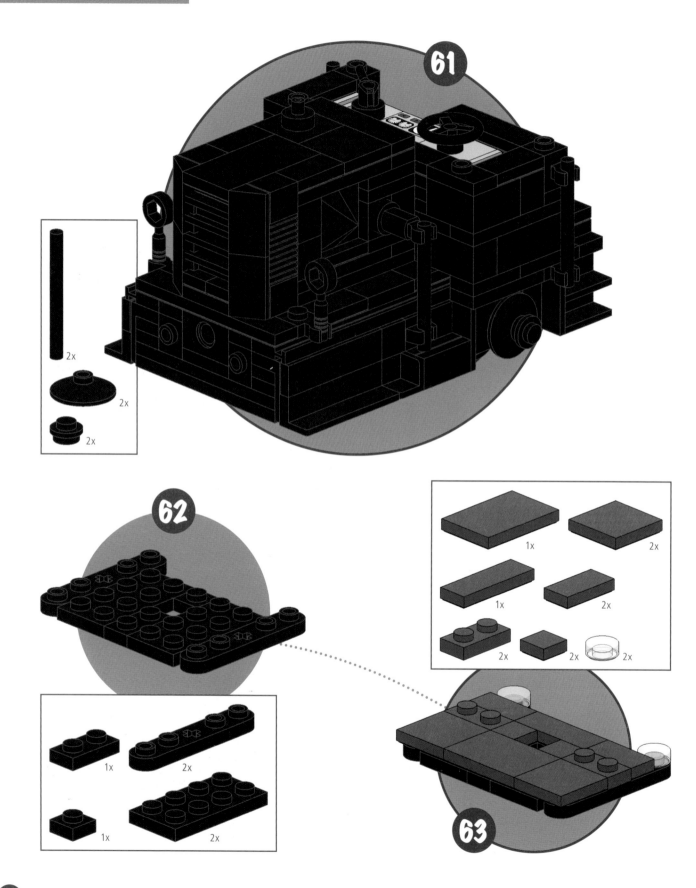

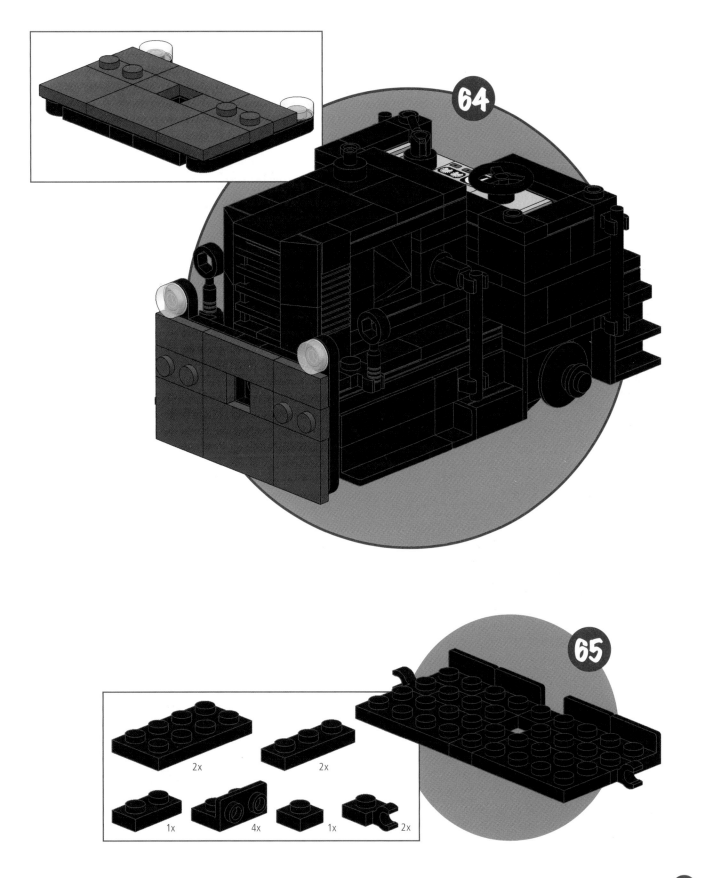

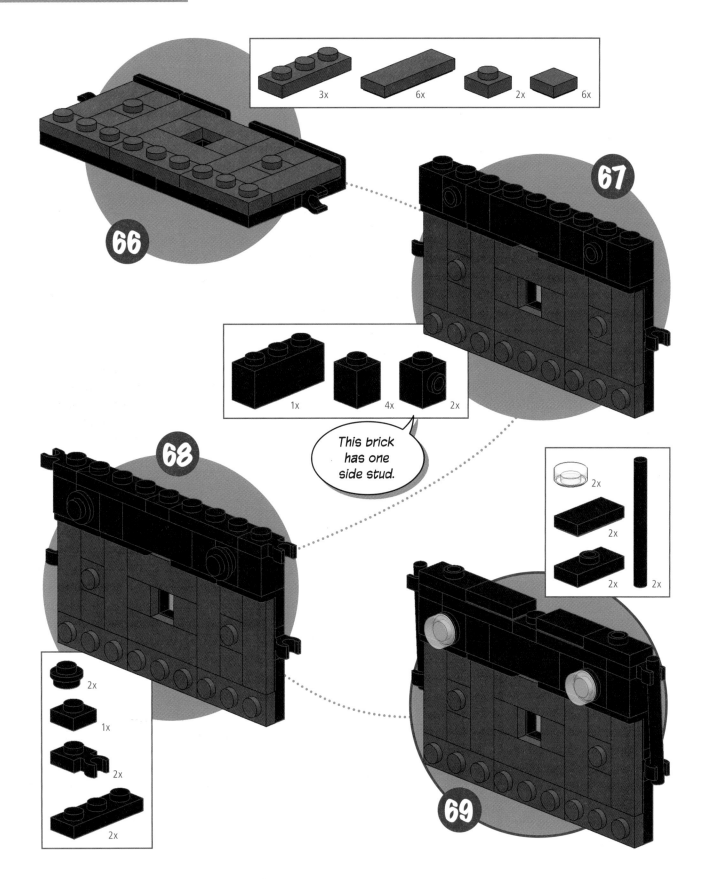

This brick
has one
side stud.

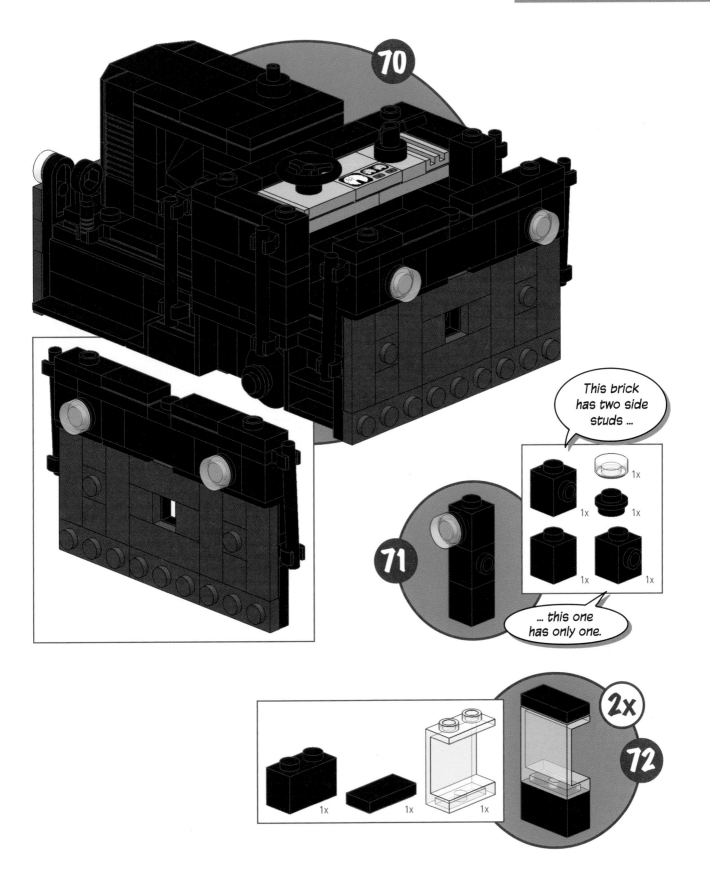

This brick has two side studs ...

... this one has only one.

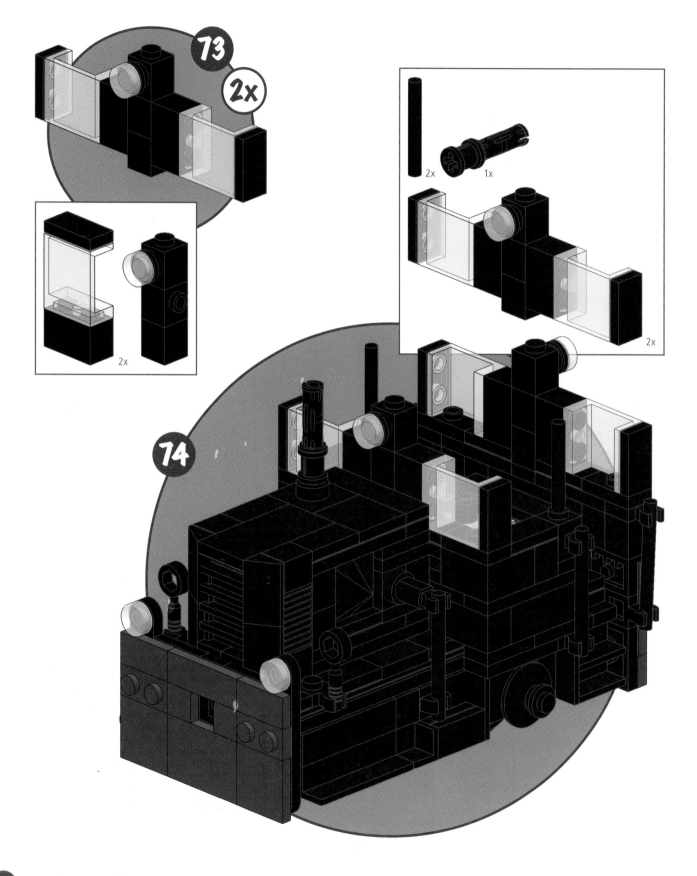

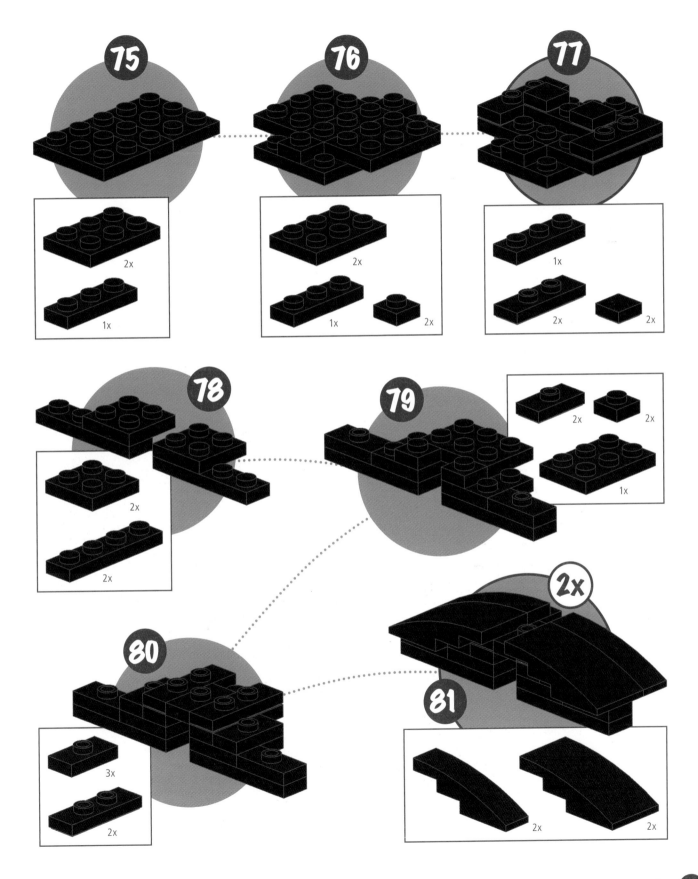

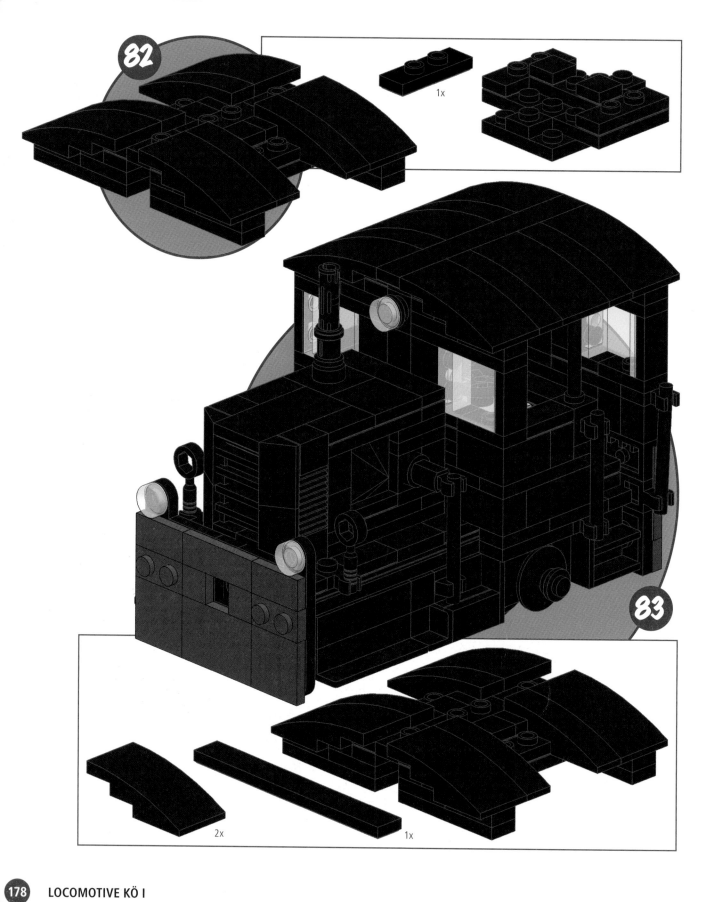

82

1x

83

2x

1x

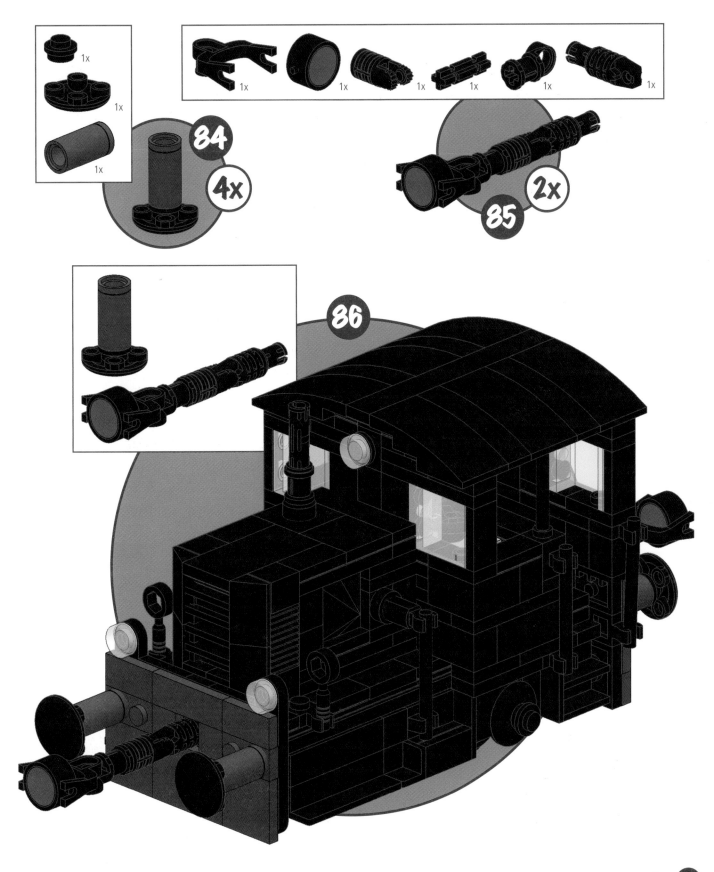

84 4x

85 2x

86

PARTS LIST

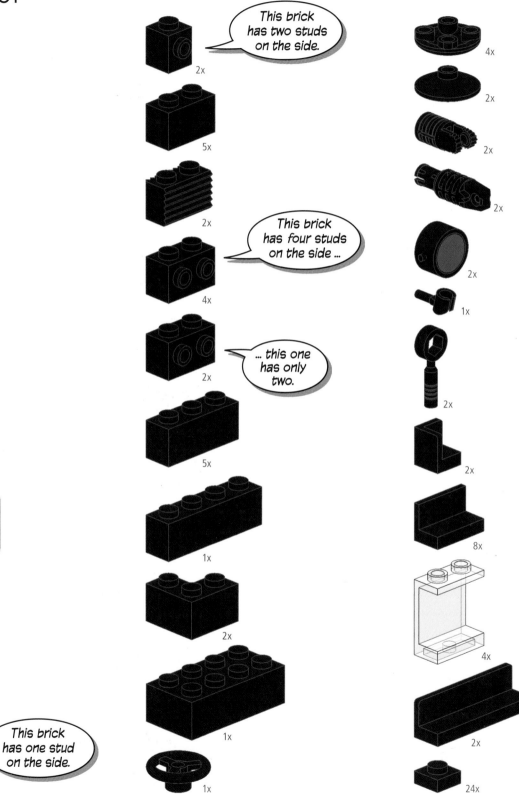

This brick has two studs on the side.

This brick has four studs on the side ...

... this one has only two.

This brick has one stud on the side.

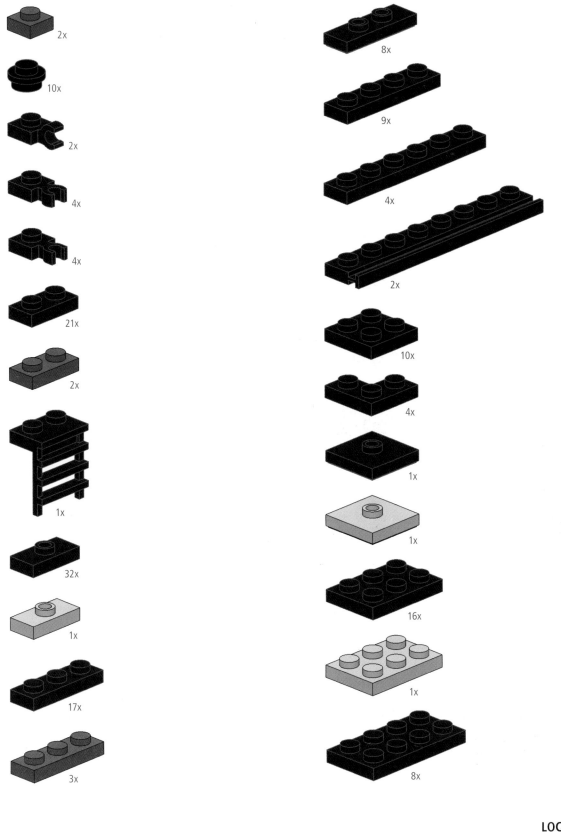

2x
10x
2x
4x
4x
21x
2x
1x
32x
1x
17x
3x

8x
9x
4x
2x
10x
4x
1x
1x
16x
1x
8x

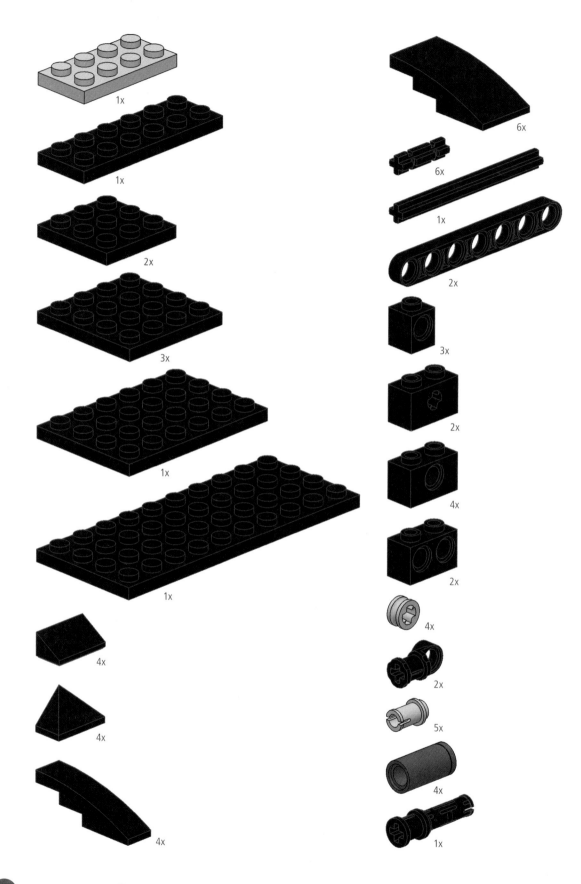

1x

1x

2x

3x

1x

1x

4x

4x

4x

6x

6x

1x

2x

3x

2x

4x

2x

4x

2x

5x

4x

1x

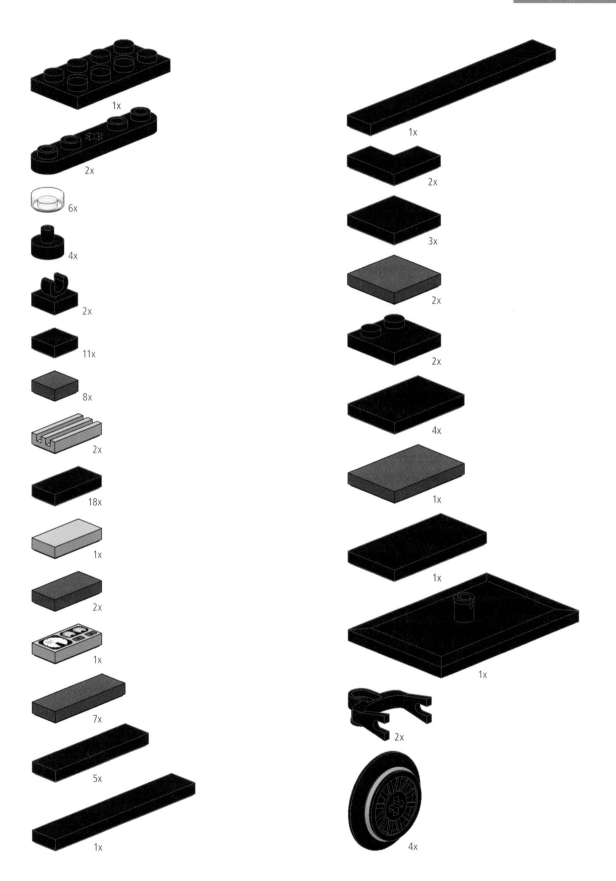

Amount	Color		Part number	Name	LEGO® Part number
2		Black	87994	Bar 3L	4566275, 4653208, 6093525
6		Black	30374	Bar 4L Lightsaber Blade	3037426, 4140303, 6116604
2		Black	11090	Bar Tube with Clip	6015891
4		Black	99780	Bracket 1 x 2 - 1 x 2 Up	6020193
2		Black	44728	Bracket 1 x 2 - 2 x 2	4184645, 4277932, 6048855, 6117973
4		Black	93274	Bracket 1 x 2 - 2 x 4	4616245, 6118829
16		Black	3005	Brick 1 x 1	300526
2		Black	30241b	Brick 1 x 1 with Clip Vertical (Thick C-Clip) and Hollow Stud	4533771
10		Black	87087	Brick 1 x 1 with Stud on 1 Side	4558954
2		Black	47905	Brick 1 x 1 with Studs on Two Opposite Sides	4214559
5		Black	3004	Brick 1 x 2	300426
2		Black	2877	Brick 1 x 2 with Grille	287726
4		Black	52107	Brick 1 x 2 with Studs on Sides	4253815
2		Black	11211	Brick 1 x 2 with Two Studs on One Side	6138173
5		Black	3622	Brick 1 x 3	362226
1		Black	3010	Brick 1 x 4	301026
2		Black	2357	Brick 2 x 2 Corner	235726
1		Black	3001	Brick 2 x 4	300126
1		Black	30663	Car Steering Wheel 2D	4153044, 6057397
4		Black	2654	Dish 2 x 2	265426, 4278359, 4617551
2		Black	4740	Dish 2 x 2 Inverted	474026
2		Black	30553	Hinge Arm Locking with Dual Finger and Axlehole	4143372
2		Black	41532	Hinge Arm Locking with Single Finger and Friction Pin	4159335
2		Black	73092	Magnet Cylindrical in Casing (Complete)	73092
1		Black	3820	Minifig Hand	
2		Black	11402i	Minifig Tool Box Wrench with 3-Rib Handle	6030875
2		Black	6231	Panel 1 x 1 x 1 Corner with Rounded Corners	4106347
8		Black	4865	Panel 1 x 2 x 1 with Square Corners	486526, 6146220
4		Trans Clear	4864b	Panel 1 x 2 x 2 with Hollow Studs	4113028, 626840
2		Black	30413	Panel 1 x 4 x 1 with Rounded Corners	4228063, 6092570
24		Black	3024	Plate 1 x 1	302426
2		Red	3024	Plate 1 x 1	302421
10		Black	4073	Plate 1 x 1 Round	614126
2		Black	61252	Plate 1 x 1 with Clip Horizontal (Thick open O-Clip)	4517925
4		Black	4085d	Plate 1 x 1 with Clip Vertical (Thick open O-Clip)	4617547
4		Black	4085b	Plate 1 x 1 with Clip Vertical (Thin U-Clip)	4550017

Amount		Color	Part number	Name	LEGO® Part number
21		Black	3023	Plate 1 x 2	302326
2		Red	3023	Plate 1 x 2	302321
1		Black	4175	Plate 1 x 2 with Ladder	4100530, 417526, 4603502
32		Black	3794a	Plate 1 x 2 without Groove with 1 Centre Stud	379426
1		Light Bluish Gray	3794a	Plate 1 x 2 without Groove with 1 Centre Stud	4211451
17		Black	3623	Plate 1 x 3	362326
3		Red	3623	Plate 1 x 3	362321
8		Black	34103	Plate 1 x 3 with 2 Studs Offset	6199908
9		Black	3710	Plate 1 x 4	371026
4		Black	3666	Plate 1 x 6	366626
2		Black	4510	Plate 1 x 8 with Door Rail	4286009
10		Black	3022	Plate 2 x 2	302226
4		Black	2420	Plate 2 x 2 Corner	242026
1		Black	87580	Plate 2 x 2 with Groove with 1 Centre Stud	4565323
1		Light Bluish Gray	87580	Plate 2 x 2 with Groove with 1 Centre Stud	4565393, 6126082
16		Black	3021	Plate 2 x 3	302126
1		Light Bluish Gray	3021	Plate 2 x 3	4211396
8		Black	3020	Plate 2 x 4	302026
1		Light Bluish Gray	3020	Plate 2 x 4	4211395
1		Black	3795	Plate 2 x 6	379526
2		Black	11212	Plate 3 x 3	6174917
3		Black	3031	Plate 4 x 4	303126, 4243819
1		Black	3032	Plate 4 x 6	303226
1		Black	3030	Plate 4 x 10	303026
4		Black	85984	Slope Brick 31 1 x 2 x 0.667	4548180
4		Black	15571	Slope Brick 45 1 x 2 Triple with Bottom Stud Holder	6051508
4		Black	61678	Slope Brick Curved 4 x 1	4522034, 6037746
6		Black	93606	Slope Brick Curved 4 x 2	4647286
6		Black	32062	Technic Axle 2 Notched	3206226, 4109810
1		Black	3706	Technic Axle 6	370626
2		Black	32065	Technic Beam 7 x 0.5	4114295
3		Black	6541	Technic Brick 1 x 1 with Hole	654126
2		Black	32064b	Technic Brick 1 x 2 with Axlehole Type 2	4233487
4		Black	3700	Technic Brick 1 x 2 with Hole	370026
2		Black	32000	Technic Brick 1 x 2 with Holes	3200026
4		Light Bluish Gray	32123a	Technic Bush 1/2 Smooth with Axle Hole Reduced	4211573
2		Black	32126	Technic Connector Toggle Joint Smooth	4660886

Amount	Color		Part number	Name	LEGO® Part number
5		Light Bluish Gray	4274	Technic Pin 1/2	4211483, 4274194
4		Red	75535	Technic Pin Joiner Round	4526984, 75854
1		Black	32054	Technic Pin Long with Stop Bush	3205426, 4107742, 4140801
1		Black	3709b	Technic Plate 2 x 4 with Holes	370926
2		Black	32124	Technic Rotor 2 Blade with 4 Studs	4114689
6		Trans Clear	98138	Tile 1 x 1 Round with Groove	4650498
4		Black	20482	Tile 1 x 1 Round with Pin and Pin Hole	6167933, 6186675
2		Black	15712	Tile 1 x 1 with Clip with Rounded Tips	6066102
11		Black	3070b	Tile 1 x 1 with Groove	307026
8		Red	3070b	Tile 1 x 1 with Groove	307021
2		Light Bluish Gray	2412b	Tile 1 x 2 Grille with Groove	4211350
18		Black	3069b	Tile 1 x 2 with Groove	306926
1		Light Bluish Gray	3069b	Tile 1 x 2 with Groove	4211414
2		Red	3069b	Tile 1 x 2 with Groove	306921
1		Light Bluish Gray	3069bpc3	Tile 1 x 2 with Red "82" and Yellow and White Gauges Pattern	
7		Red	63864	Tile 1 x 3 with Groove	4533742
5		Black	2431	Tile 1 x 4 with Groove	243126
1		Black	6636	Tile 1 x 6	663626
1		Black	4162	Tile 1 x 8	416226
2		Black	14719	Tile 2 x 2 Corner	6133722
3		Black	3068b	Tile 2 x 2 with Groove	306826
2		Red	3068b	Tile 2 x 2 with Groove	306821
2		Black	33909	Tile 2 x 2 with Studs on Edge	6192346
4		Black	26603	Tile 2 x 3	6162892
1		Red	26603	Tile 2 x 3	6189130
1		Black	87079	Tile 2 x 4 with Groove	4560182
1		Black	4025	Train Bogie Plate with Short Pin	402526, 6051914, 6096842
2		Black	2920	Train Coupling Type 2	4299239
4		Black	55423	Train Wheel for RC Train w Technic Axle Hole and Rubber Ring	4289864, 4582034, 4621116

▉HATCH & HANDLE

This door is an interesting example of an npu (*BL 87601 / LEGO® 4561944 or 6074916*). Uwe installed it as a loading hatch for this freight car.

And while we're on the subject of doors and hatches, the Injection Syringe (*BL 87989 / LEGO® 4563719*) inserted into an inverted Technic Pin ½ (*BL 4274 / LEGO® 4211483 or 4274194*) makes a great door handle.

MORE NICE PART USAGE

On the next pages we would like to show you some more "unusual" tips, so to speak.

▍ BUMPER CAR

Let's get back to the fair! Aren't the little bumper cars cute?

As you can see, they are quite easy to put together. The crucial part is a big old car tire (*BL 36*), which you have to pull over right at the end. It's a bit tricky to position it without holding all the pieces in one hand, but we think the result is worth it.

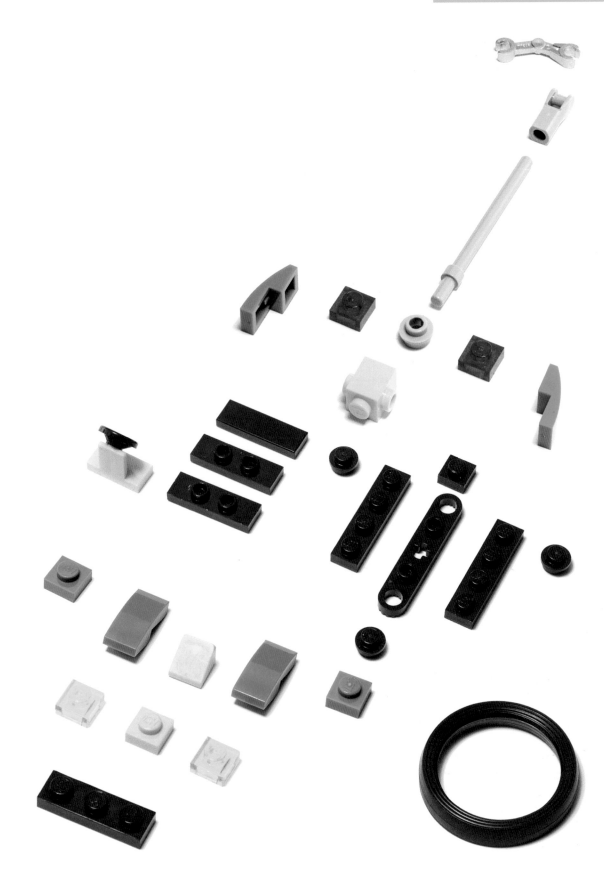

SMOKEBOX

You've also seen the same tires in use for Uwe's steam engine: It makes a great frame for the door of the smokebox.

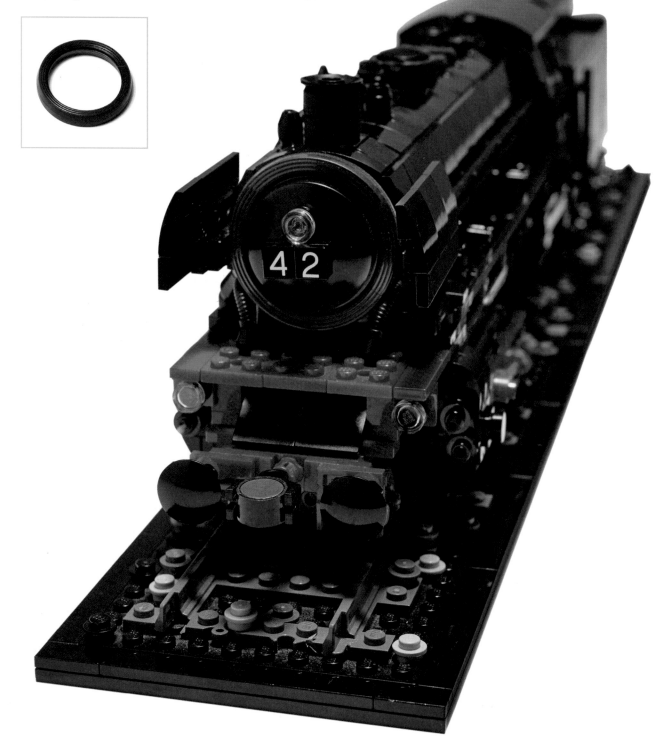

SPINNER CAR

You can also do a lot more with it. For example, I pulled one over the front of my model of the Spinner cars from the movie Blade Runner (*1982*).

GARAGE DOOR

A nice element that can make your model look much more realistic is the Flex Rod 11M (*BL 32199 / LEGO®4141973*). Here is an example of it covering a garage door from the inside.

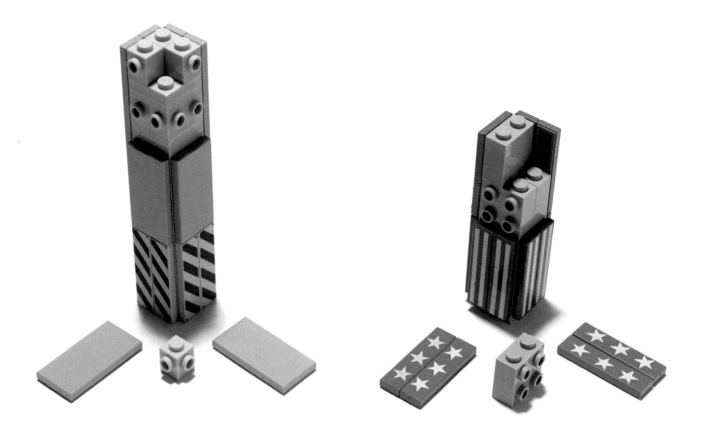

■ COLUMNS

You can make columns quite easily with snot bricks *(studs not on top)* this makes for beautifully smooth tiles. We used the column on the left in our underground parking lot, and the one on the right in our bumper car scene.

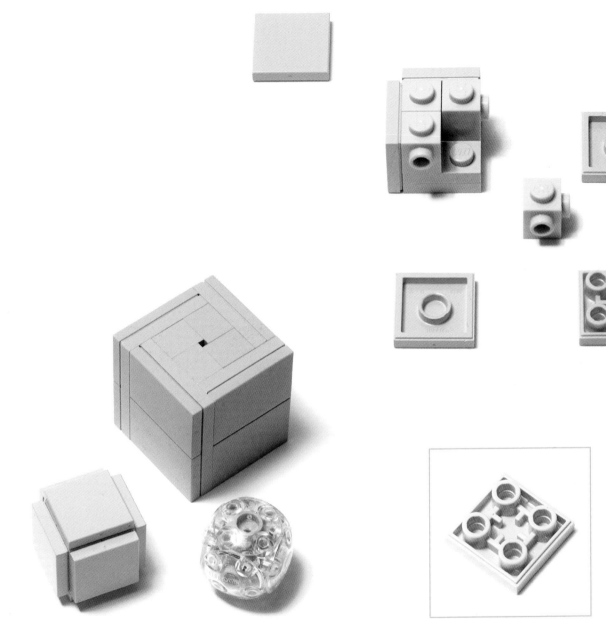

BOXES

Boxes can be built according to the same principle:For the underside of the small pink box, you need an inverse 2x2 tile (*BL11203 / LEGO® 6101937*).

For the next size up, you can make the box with a figure-stand (*BL 88646 / LEGO® 6079461*) and 2x3 Flat Tiles (*BL 26603 / LEGO® 6171894*).

MORE NICE PART USAGE 195

▍BALL

The ball follows the same pattern, but is a little trickier, because you have to turn the flowers (*BL 33291 / LEGO® 6182167*) to face each other so that all six sliding plates (*BL 2654 / LEGO® 4199303 or 4278412*) interlock.

LETTERING

Building letters and complete words or slogans with LEGO® bricks is always a challenge. However, the many elements available can also offer unexpected possibilities for a wide variety of solutions in a wide range of lettering styles.

For the lettering in Mel's Diner we used Inverted 2x2 Flat Tiles (*BL 11203 / LEGO® 6132886*) and Plates with Half Bow Inverted 1X2x2/3 (*BL 24201 / LEGO® 6144138*). If you look closely, you can see the place where we snotted bricks in the wall.

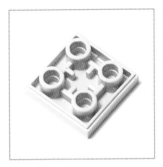  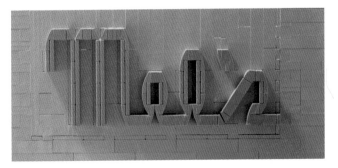

For our ambulance, we used a type of block lettering, and it is also snotted.

This perspective of our Waffle Hat lets you take a peek "behind the scenes," for example, of the tubes that serve as spacers and stabilize tiles without a firm connection. They ensure that the lettering sticks out a bit at the front and creates a nice three-dimensional effect.

Even if you only have three rows for a marquee, you can still create words. Unfortunately, you can't get all letters on red tiles. So, for my sign, I had to come up with a "movie title" that would work with the letters available.

By the way, the glass bricks are old dark-gray 2x2 bricks with printing (*BL 3003px1*).

Below this you can see an example of how you can build freestanding letters. Nice and colorful, aren't they?

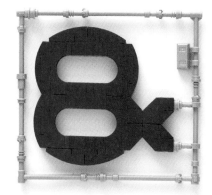

Based on the model cast frame, we also constructed this book's title. The frame makes it possible to integrate other elements. You can, of course, let the lettering work for itself.

If you stay with this topic for a while, it gradually becomes easier to recreate real existing fonts or even logos. Have a go! We're sure that you'll come up with something.

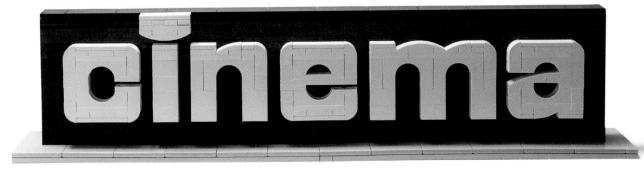

As a child of the 1990s, I personally found trying to build the logo for Game Boy Color an exciting challenge. Of course, it shouldn't be included here only as decoration. We'll take a closer look at it and show you our solution for its construction.

MAGIC CUBE

And of course we can't leave out the "magic cube" from the theme of "nostalgic trend toys." We assembled it from 27 dice (*BL 64776*) from LEGO® games.

STICKERS

As in our last book on tricks with LEGO®, we will now show you some sticker sheets that can be very helpful.
You can find them, e.g. at Bricklink, by the number at the bottom of the sheets.

22637

RECYCL

WARNING

NO ENTRY

SUPER SECRET

POLICE

ST
43

ST
43

ST43

GOOD WORK

16447/6061095 © 2014 LEGO GROUP

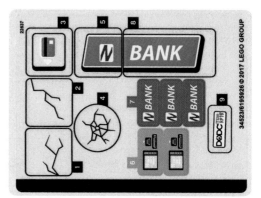

22637

BANK

BANK BANK BANK

34523/6195926 © 2017 LEGO GROUP

22637

JC60082   ER60082

RK60082   ER60082

33 33

33

DUNE RANGER

19277/6097575 © 2015 LEGO GROUP

22637

60009   60009

POLICE

POLICE

POLICE

POLICE
60007

POLICE
60007

POLICE
60007

POLICE

POLICE

POLICE

GH60007

12751/6021254 © 2013 LEGO GROUP

55027/4287825 © 2006 LEGO GROUP

56026/4296371 © 2006 LEGO GROUP

POLICE

POLICE

POLICE

POLICE   S6-8004

-5472

HIGHWAY PATROL

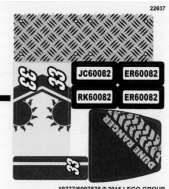

World Unity
FESTIVAL

World Unity
FESTIVAL

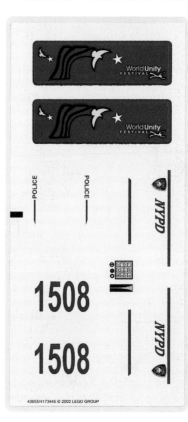

POLICE

POLICE

NYPD

1508

NYPD

1508

43655/4173445 © 2002 LEGO GROUP

22637

1

RESCUE

RESCUE

DANGER

DANGER

3

6

5

4

2

16026/6056837 © 2014 LEGO GROUP

7239   FEUERWEHR   FIRE

7239   FEUERWEHR   FIRE

52888/4262483 © 2005 LEGO GROUP